In the Centre Lies Virtue

A short, no nonsense guide to who you are, where you came from and how to be happy.

Vincent Kennedy

Copyright Vincent Kennedy 2016

Website: Vincent-kennedy.com
Facebook: Vincent Kennedy Art
Twitter: @Cahore1509

Contents

Preface 7

Introduction 13

Life

Chapter 1: From Dust 23

Chapter 2: Well I'll be a Monkeys Uncle 31

Faith

Chapter 3: Foundations Built on Sand 43

Chapter 4: 'Blind' Faith 59

Death

Chapter 5: And to Dust You Shall Return 71

Happiness

Chapter 6: The Holy Grail 83

Chapter 7: Taking Control 93

Chapter 8: Our Driving Forces 103

Chapter 9: Be More Stoic 115

Chapter 10: Revelations 129

Acknowledgements 145

Further Reading / Viewing 147

For my children.

That they may be free of anxiety, free of pain, free of superstition - and fearless in their endeavours.

Preface

This book was born out of a few things. I have always had, even from a very young age, an underlying anxiety and confusion about life. I never really knew what was real. I was bewildered with life and my role within this world. This confusion caused me to be depressed, and for the last 20 years, have regular thoughts of suicide and death.

I could not help but notice that depression, and indeed suicide, seemed to be a systemic problem. A problem not just for 'vulnerable people' or addicts, or the psychotic, but right across all sections of society apparently striking without bias toward any cultural group. The only distinct group with significantly increased numbers is young to middle aged males, which includes me.

Depression is a common illness worldwide, with an estimated 350 million people affected. Depression is different from usual mood fluctuations and short-lived emotional responses to challenges in everyday life. Especially when long-lasting and with moderate or severe intensity, depression may become a serious health condition. It can cause the affected person to suffer greatly and function poorly at work, at school and in the family and relationships in general.

Close to 1 million people die due to suicide every year and there are many more who attempt suicide. Hence, many millions of people are affected or experience suicide bereavement every year. Suicide occurs throughout the lifespan and was the second leading cause of death among

15-29 year olds globally in 2012. Suicide accounted for 1.4% of all deaths worldwide, making it the 15th leading cause of death in 2012.

As the French philosopher Albert Camus said, "There is but one truly serious philosophical problem, and that is suicide..."

I wanted to find out what the hell was going on! What was life all about anyway? What does it mean to be human? What does one's existence actually mean? And why do so many people, including myself at one time, want to end their own lives?
  A big reason that I decided to put pen to paper was that I searched for years for answers but there is so much pseudoscience and nonsense out there. We lap up this pseudoscience and nonsense as 'truth' because it's what we want to hear - it validates our *confirmation bias*.
I analyse four major areas of the human experience that affect our understanding of our own existence. They are:

<u>Life</u>: The truth of what we are and where we come from.
<u>Faith</u>: What does faith actually mean and where did it come from?
<u>Death</u>: Its effects on our actual lives.
<u>Happiness</u>: What does it take, and mean, to be happy? Emphasis will be placed on happiness and fulfilment, as it is, or should be, our goal.

When I was depressed and suicidal I had a really deep feeling that I was running away from something, that something terribly bad was happening, or going to happen to me. It turns out that indeed *I was* running away from something, but to my surprise, I've learned, *we are all running away from the same thing.*

"Nothing, Everything, Anything, Something: If you have nothing, then you have everything, because you have the freedom to do anything, without the fear of losing something"
                    Jarod Kintz

Introduction

"To be what we are, and to become what we are capable of, is the only end of life"

Robert Louis Stevenson

"Your fears are a kind of prison that confines you within a limited range of action. The less you fear, the more power you will have and the more fully you will live."

Robert Green

We all have a yearning within us to be the best we can be and live the fullest possible life we can. However, this journey appears to be fraught with fear and danger. We have no choice but to be born in the time and place that we are. We did not *decide* to be here. Your parents may have chosen to have a child, but no one was to know - it was going to be *you*. You could have been born in any time, any place throughout history, but this happens to be your time - right now.

Our parents, once they had us, gave us a multitude of ideas and tried to teach us various lessons. Of course they meant well, but even some of these well meaning ideas can have catastrophic negative effects. Old out dated philosophies and superstitions can seep deeply into our subconscious making it *almost* impossible to change these ideas as we get older.

What was 'true' when we were children, was what we were told. However this can be manipulated to mould us, rather than let us find out the truth of our world through self discovery, using our own critical thinking and innate curiosities. We are reared with blinkers on, oblivious to the wonders and magnificence of the world, the universe, and especially ourselves. It is only when we remove these blinkers and critically assess ourselves, and our world, that we can decide what role *we want* to play in it. As Robert Green says; "The world *wants* to assign you a role in life. And once you accept that role, you are doomed."

We think (are taught) that education must be the answer to a happy life. A sound education provides a platform to which we advance into a decent career, with a decent salary, and then have the security and funds to provide for our own children. I've found education has become very little more than acquirement of data, that is to be regurgitated at exam time. Students with a good memory should do exceptionally well. Are we taught about our feelings, about the workings of our mind or how to critically assess our world? As Bertrand Russell said, "we are faced with the paradoxical fact that education has become one of the chief obstacles to intelligence and freedom of thought."

Education does give us goals and a purpose as we are growing up. We want to do well and achieve decent results, or educate ourselves in a certain trade. As each year passes more targets are in place to occupy our thoughts and energies. The problem of existence may then hit home after that, when we no longer have these goals set in front of us – we have nothing at which to aim going forward. We have attained the job, the career that we had been aiming for, or that maybe someone else had been guiding us toward – but what next?

A certain amount of emptiness may arise if you're *not* in a role that you truly wanted. A significant amount of fear and anxiety can be produced by these realisations. To turn your back on something you've tried hard (or even not that hard) to get, may feel completely unfeasible. But you have to be willing to change *everything*. Even the feeling that you're willing to change everything gives you more freedom and less fear within the thing you're actually doing or the role you have 'accepted'.

This fear, along with a whole host of others can cripple our potential. We are born with *only* two innate fears: the fear of falling and the fear of loud noises. All the others are learned; fear of change; fear of acceptance; fear of failure; fear of rejection; fear of making a fool of yourself; fear of public speaking and even the fears like that of spiders and snakes etc; they are all learned - and can be unlearned!

Our fears and anxieties can be so overwhelming, so overpowering that we may think that *only* 'Divine' intervention will change them. We get this idea from indoctrination of religious beliefs from a very young age. We live in a 'religious' community or cultural setting where the idea of a God is just the way things are, where every single person you know believes in this deity, so why would *you* ever think of questioning it? We are taught that there is this 'being' that looks after us, cares for us and is guiding us through our lives. It is almost impossible to let this belief go because life is scary, life is frightening and we are taught to have hope that this God will look after us. What use is hope if it abdicates our responsibility for caution, scepticism and most importantly our action!

It is action that changes things; it is action that gets you where you need to be. There is a certain amount of mysticism around the 'talent' we see on TV. Be that sports people, or singers, actors, musicians, scientists or engineers. It was not *just* talent that got them there, it was not *just* luck, and it was not *just* good fortune. It was bloody hard work - hours and hours cultivating their craft to get to the top of their chosen professions - 10,000 hours (in fact) is the magical number says Malcolm Gladwell in his book *Outliers*. Any real achievement takes huge amounts of dedication, commitment, will power and perseverance. If you want something, you have to be willing to work your ass off to get it – are you willing?

In this world of high technology, where everything seems to need to be done faster and more efficiently we are missing the only important thing that can truly give you happiness – the present moment. It's actually all that we have. As the Scottish psychiatrist R.D. Laing puts it, "We live in a moment of history where change is so speeded up that we begin to see the present only when it is already disappearing."

We may continually torment ourselves with self loathing about past events or fear and dread about the future. Conversely, we may think about how great we were, or how great we are going to be. Either way the present moment is lost, wasted, and not to be had again. We *do* have plenty of time though. As Seneca, the stoic philosopher, said "It is not that we have so little time but that we lose so much.... The life we receive is not short but we make it so; we are not ill provided but use what we have wastefully."

We need to take responsibility for our time *and* responsibility for ourselves! How often do we sit and grumble over the 'cards we are dealt' or the situation in which we find ourselves? Is it not true that we mostly blame other things, other people or lost opportunities and stay in the slump we are in *expecting* things to change? Expecting - without action. It's action that we need to change things, to improve our situation and be the humans we should ultimately be.

We don't need to be preoccupied with the results, but just to try something that we want to try – forgetting everyone else. We cannot simply accept a role to fit in, and to not 'rock the boat'. It's the people who 'rocked the boat' that have changed history but we only have to be ourselves to have the effect we want in our own world. If you listen hard enough to yourself, and work at things you like doing - you will *know* who you are. However this is only the start because it can take a lot of courage (and other virtues) to *be* who you are instead of just fitting in. As the author and life coach Vironika Tugaleva said, "Who was I fooling, telling my heart to quiet its beautiful song so I could march in the parade of conformity? My biggest fool was me."

Things that are left unsaid and are indeed supposedly unquestionable pose our biggest problems and cause most of our confusion. Everything must be put on the table and open for deliberation and discussion. To find the answers to our biggest questions, our biggest problems, we must be fearless in our inquiry and truthful with our findings.

LIFE

The condition that distinguishes animals and plants from inorganic matter, including the capacity for growth, reproduction, functional activity, and continual change preceding death.

Chapter 1

From Dust

"Because there is a law such as gravity, the Universe can and will create itself from nothing. Spontaneous creation is the reason there is something rather than nothing, why the Universe exists, why we exist. It is not necessary to invoke God to light the blue touch paper and set the Universe going."

Stephen Hawking

"All you really need to know for the moment is that the universe is a lot more complicated than you might think, even if you start from a position of thinking it's pretty damn complicated in the first place."
Douglas Adams

To begin this story of where we are now, and why we are the way we are, we have to go back, right back to the very beginning of time itself. To understand our psychology it is vital that we discuss the beginnings of our universe.

The word awesome gets thrown around a lot but the universe, the cosmos, as Carl Sagan puts it, "which is all that is, or was, or ever will be", is truly awesome and truly epic in its size and scale. So much so that when you hear the numbers involved they are incomprehensible. We have nothing else, even remotely close, with which to make a comparison. The knowledge about our universe (and our species) has come about through scientific endeavours so I will therefore have to discuss, in the early chapters and as reader friendly as I can, the science of life.

The best estimate for the age of the universe by physicists is 13.8 billion years. Now obviously this figure was not plucked out of the air, it is calculated using the model of the evolution of the universe from the Big Bang. Using the model, it is understood where in the model we are now and extrapolating backwards to when the universe was a singularity, or at a single point. To put it very simply, the universe is expanding (the further away the faster it is moving) and if it is expanding, then (using intricate mathematics) it can be shown to have been at the one single point – The Big Bang i.e. the beginning of time itself.

But what was the Big Bang? Well at the singularity all the mass that occupies the universe now, was at this one singular, infinitesimally small point. As Bill Bryson states in *A Short History of Nearly Everything*, 'the singularity has no around, around it. There is no space for it to occupy, no place for it to be. We can't even ask how long it has been there – whether it has just lately popped into being, like a good idea, or whether it has been there forever, quietly awaiting the right moment. Time doesn't exist. There is no past for it to emerge from.' The next line from Bill is the really important one; 'And so from nothing, our universe begins.'

Bryson also writes of the Big Bang; 'not to think of it as an explosion in the conventional sense' but rather that it was 'a vast, sudden expansion on a whopping scale.' The universe was extremely hot at this stage, about 10 billion degrees Kelvin, and in 'less than one minute the universe is a million billion miles across and growing fast.' Space itself expanded faster than the speed of light.

The light elements; hydrogen, helium and a dusting of lithium, were born during the first 3 minutes. NASA says that for the next roughly 380,000 years very little happened (it was too hot), until at this point the matter cooled, resulting in the formation of a 'transparent, electrically neutral gas'. Things started to get really interesting after about 400 million years, because after this, and lasting about half-billion years, temperatures dropped enough for these gas clouds to collapse to form the first generation of stars and galaxies. As Johnny B Truant says in his humorous and inspiring post, *The Universe Doesn't Give a Flying Fuck About You,* 'You know.... to "cool down" enough to become giant fucking balls of fire.'

But what about closer to home, like our solar system and of course our planet earth? Our solar system did not form until another 9 billion years after the Big Bang. Our solar system, and earth included, is approx 4.5 billion years old. It was formed due to the gravitational collapse of the small part of a giant molecular cloud. Most of the mass collected at the centre forming our sun, with the rest flattening into a protoplanetary disk. It was from this disk that the planets within the solar system formed. As each planet grew, the force of gravity increased and drew more and more clumps toward them, until eventually all the planets were formed.

Our star, the sun, is of fairly average size and the planets (including ours sitting in the goldilocks zone- being not too hot and not too cold for carbon based life) spin round it in elliptical orbits – heliocentric model. Laws of mathematics govern the elliptical orbits of the planets and everything in the universe, but this seemed to pose a problem to the now famous Napoleon Bonaparte. He asked the French scientist Pierre-Simon Laplace where God, or the Creator, fitted into this model. Laplace answered bluntly, *"Je n'avais pas besoin de cette hypothèse-là."* It simply translates as "I had no need for that hypothesis".

This solar system is on one spiral arm of the Milky Way galaxy. 'Current estimates suggest that our galaxy has approx 400 billion stars, and up to 50 billion planets. If even 1% of those are in their systems goldilocks zones, then there are over 500 million planets in our galaxy alone capable of supporting life.' The Milky Way is also spinning and it takes 225 million years to do one rotation; the last time our solar system was in its current position dinosaurs were just beginning to roam the earth!

There are approx 100 billion other galaxies (at least) within the observable universe. The universe is also so vast that distances are calculated in light years; one light year is the distance that light travels in one year and is the equivalent to nearly 6 trillion miles. Certainly not any distance we would be travelling in the near future. Our nearest galaxy, Andromeda, is 2.5 million light years away which means; 2.5 million x 6 trillion miles away, and that's our neighbour!

A simple but also astounding fact is that when we look at the night sky we are literally looking back in time. Take Andromeda for example, as I have mentioned it already. As astronomers look at Andromeda they don't see it as it is, they see it as it was, 2.5 million years ago! Also as we look at something much closer, like our sun, we see it as it was 8 minutes ago.

Our galaxy is approx 100,000 light years across (100,000 x 6 trillion miles across) and to remind you this is one of 100+ billion galaxies. Developments within theoretical physics are also pointing toward our universe being just one of many universes in a multiverse. Think of bubbles in a bath. Our universe would be just one of those bubbles. The whole thing is mind boggling!

The most fascinating thing about the universe is not that we are a part of it, but that it is a part of us. You see stars are not just bright points of light in the night sky that are pretty to look at. They are giant burning fires that create different atoms during their lifetime, in a process called stellar nucleosynthesis. Most of the chemical elements seen on the periodic table (remember that poster in chemistry class) were either formed during this nuclear fusion in large stars, or during the stars death, in the supernovae explosion.

These elements were also scattered during the explosion and form the next generation of gas clouds and planets. The atoms that comprise everything, including your body, were created billions of years ago and trillions of miles away by stars. In fact "the atoms in your left hand probably came from different stars than the atoms in your right hand." So as Lawrence Krauss puts it, "Jesus didn't die for you, stars did, you are here today because of stars."

Our sun is one of these stars and it too has its lifespan. It's actually about half way through its life and in due course it will reach its end. Even if our species did survive until this time, which I highly doubt, that will be the end of planet earth and everything on it. Would a great designer really have placed his most prized creation in an indistinct corner of the cosmos, survival hinging on a star that will in the future, expand across our solar system as a *red giant* frying everything in its path before fizzling down to a *white dwarf?*

On a much larger scale, Andromeda and the Milky Way are on a collision course and they will collide to form a much larger galaxy. The physics shows all these things happening under natural conditions, through natural processes, with no obvious sign of any magisterial influence. George Smoot, an astrophysicist, cosmologist and a Nobel Prize winner for physics in 2006, said "when people really understand the Big Bang and the whole sweep of the evolution of the universe, it will be clear that humans are fairly insignificant."

Chapter 2

Well, I'll be a Monkey's Uncle.

"We must, however, acknowledge, as it seems to me, that man with all his noble qualities... still bears in his bodily frame the indelible stamp of his lowly origin."

Charles Darwin

"The theory of evolution, like the theory of gravity, is a scientific fact"

Neil deGrasse Tyson

So we are on a lump of rock, orbiting a medium sized star in the back corner of an incomprehensibly huge universe. But how did we, the human species arrive here? Well the answer to that question is, for me, simply the greatest scientific finding of all time. The answer is evolution.

Evolution by means of natural selection was first described by Charles Darwin, and Alfred Russel Wallace in the work, *On the Origin of Species* in 1859. Evolution could be deduced by very simple observations of plants and animals it was controversial at the time, but it is now one of the best understood and well documented areas within biology. Evolution has nothing to do with the origin of life but once life started it was evolution that produced all the variety of plants and animals we see today. In fact over 99.9% of species that ever lived have become extinct.

The exact way in which life started is only a hypothesis at this stage but we know that all the chemical elements necessary for life were present in abundance. Even with the ingredients present, it still took a billion years after the earth formed for life to start. The first life would have been simple single celled organisms (evolved through chemical evolution) that were able to self replicate at a greater rate than the rate the organism died. Once this happened then evolution took over and all the branches in the tree of life began to grow.

The first mutlicellular life started about 900 million years ago, the first animals around half a billion years ago and the first 'modern humans' or Homo Sapiens, around 200 thousand years ago. We have only been here for a tiny fraction of time in comparison to the other life on earth - it's almost like we've crashed their party.

The real important branch (for us) on the tree of life is of course our own. As far as being alive we are no different than any other species on the planet. We are on the tree of life along with everything else and our relationship to other animals is undeniable. If people can't handle the fact we are related to monkeys, how are they going to feel when they realise we are related to a dung beetle, or an oak tree? We are part of the beauty of life on earth.

We are special in so far as we have the ability to understand our world and make life better for ourselves and future generations. We can adapt our environment to suit us, we have an opportunity to learn and improve, to investigate and explore, to love and care for one another. The latter is especially relevant as we know that every one of the approximately 7 billion people on this planet are part of one species, all of us are brothers and sisters clinging to a vulnerable existence.

Considering what this planet has been through in its long history its surprising that life still exists, let alone that *we* were able to evolve. One example was the period about 700 million years ago called 'Snowball Earth' when the planet was almost completely covered in a huge layer of ice, up to 3kms thick. Small organisms were tough enough to survive this period and everything else from then on owes their existence to that toughness and durability. Another example of life's vulnerability is probably the best known event in the history of the planet; the extinction of the dinosaurs. Everyone, I'm sure, has heard about it in some instance or another.

Dinosaurs were the dominant species on this planet for over 135 million years until about 65 million years ago. The best explanation for their extinction was a 3-9 mile wide meteor or bolide impact near Mexico. The Chelyabinsk meteor in 2013 that can easily be seen on YouTube is a *slight* visual example of what snuffed the dinosaurs, only its predecessor was on a massively increased scale. The 110 mile wide Chicxulub crater that was left behind by the dinosaur destroying impact can still be seen to this day.

The impact not only ended the long dominant run of the dinosaurs but changed the face of life on this planet forever, especially for us. For who knows, if that meteor had not hit, the dinosaurs may still be lords of the earth, and the mammal group that we evolved from would have followed a very different evolutionary path. However, the dinosaurs did die out and an opportunity was created for the early mammals to thrive, evolve and create a whole new species - one of which was to lead to us.

We belong to a specific group of ape, the hominid. About 50,000 years ago there may still have been four similar species of hominid living along side us but we are the only group of hominid to survive. From a scientific standpoint we *are* actually apes and share 98.6% of our DNA with chimps. I can already hear people say, "if we came from monkeys, then why are there still monkeys?"

We did not descend from monkeys - we share a common ancestor with them. That common ancestor lived some 5 to 7 million years ago with the chimps following a different evolutionary path that us. We have 23 pairs of chromosomes compared to chimpanzees 24 pairs. Therefore, if we are so closely related, how did this happen? The hypothesis was that one pair of chromosomes must have fused to reduce the overall number of pairs by one, and indeed this was the case with chromosome 2. This was further tested in 2005 when they sequenced the chimpanzee genome and compared it to the human genome. Chromosome 2 could be matched to 2 unfused chromosomes in the chimpanzee genome! Pretty cool stuff!

We are not free from the threat of extinction either and have had close calls in the past. One such *bottleneck* in population size is believed to be due to the Toba super volcano about 75 thousand years ago, which caused a drastic climate change that could have been our undoing. It is estimated that the population of humans was down as low as 600 breeding individuals. That could have been it, shows over, lights out, erased from time. But our ancestors did survive and every one of the 7 billion people on this planet are descendants of, and owe their existence to, that small, but very tough group of hunter gatherers.

We are one of the results of a long history of organisms fighting for survival, unconsciously fine tuning themselves to their environment and developing into newer more adaptive life forms. These adaptations includes improved photosynthesisers, more cunning hunters, more elusive prey, faster swimmers, more acrobatic flyers, and for us vastly improved cognitive abilities. Flora and fauna are so well adapted to their environment that it would have seemed to the infantile and ignorant populace of our earlier ancestors, that these life forms were indeed, 'created'. They could not have known or understood the 'bottom up' development undergone by these species over an immense period of time. However this is no longer the case and we now know the history of man, and of course, his 'lowly origins'.

One way to think about it is this: Think of a puddle suddenly becoming conscious of 'itself'. It would be amazed at how it fits perfectly into its pothole in the road. It would assume that the pothole must have been *created* for it; it's just such a perfect match. But as with us, and our environment, the puddle came second and has no choice *but* to fit into the pothole!

The natural development of our universe, our solar system, and indeed us, for me answers a very important question about purpose – there appears to be no purpose. It is not rational that there is a universe let alone a species that can supposedly rationally assess that irrational universe! There is no big secret, no path you have to follow, no set rules you have to obey and no one you have to answer to but yourself. The meaning therefore of life is whatever you choose it to be.

We all have a small window of opportunity from birth until death to do and be whatever we decide for ourselves. There is no room for pride, fear or worry, jealousy or resentment, anger or bitterness. The simple most important thing in any humans' life is time. Why waste it with negative or indeed fruitless endeavours when you can use your time to learn, to improve, to love, to create, to laugh and to follow whatever purpose that you decide to give your life.

The spectacular freedom and unbelievable opportunity we have as thinking beings could be magnificent with scientific knowledge guiding us along the way. However there is one huge problem that has piggy backed its way along on our psychological evolutionary adaptations. That problem is religion (and our propensity to believing other superstitious rubbish!).

I want to introduce you to some words from Carl Sagan before I leave the discussion about life. Carl has taught more about the beauty of life, and the folly of our species, than anyone else. The following excerpt is taken from his book *Pale Blue Dot: A Vision of the Human Future in Space*. The title comes from an image taken of earth, from 6 billion kilometres away, by the Voyager 1 space probe on February 24, 1990.

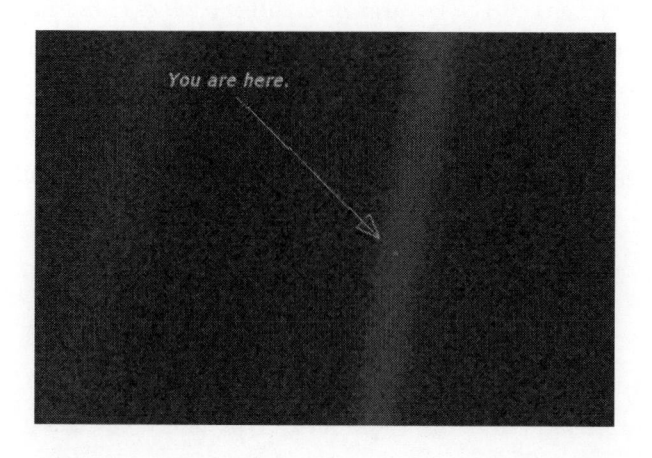

"Look again at that dot. That's here. That's home. That's us. On it everyone you love, everyone you know, everyone you ever heard of, every human being who ever was, lived out their lives. The aggregate of our joy and suffering, thousands of confident religions, ideologies, and economic doctrines, every hunter and forager, every hero and coward, every creator and destroyer of civilization, every king and peasant, every young couple in love, every mother and father, hopeful child, inventor and explorer, every teacher of morals, every corrupt politician, every "superstar," every "supreme leader," every saint and sinner in the history of our species lived there-on a mote of dust suspended in a sunbeam.

The Earth is a very small stage in a vast cosmic arena. Think of the endless cruelties visited by the inhabitants of one corner of this pixel on the scarcely distinguishable inhabitants of some other corner, how frequent their misunderstandings, how eager they are to kill one another, how fervent their hatreds. Think of the rivers of blood spilled by all those generals and emperors so that, in glory and triumph, they could become the momentary masters of a fraction of a dot.

Our posturings, our imagined self-importance, the delusion that we have some privileged position in the Universe, are challenged by this point of pale light. Our planet is a lonely speck in the great enveloping cosmic dark. In our obscurity, in all this vastness, there is no hint that help will come from elsewhere to save us from ourselves.

The Earth is the only world known so far to harbour life. There is nowhere else, at least in the near future, to which our species could migrate. Visit, yes. Settle, not yet. Like it or not, for the moment the Earth is where we make our stand.

It has been said that astronomy is a humbling and character-building experience. There is perhaps no better demonstration of the folly of human conceits than this distant image of our tiny world. To me, it underscores our responsibility to deal more kindly with one another, and to preserve and cherish the pale blue dot, the only home we've ever known."

FAITH

Strong belief in the doctrines of a religion, based on spiritual conviction rather than proof.

Chapter 3

Foundations Built on Sand

"The whole thing is so patently infantile, so foreign to reality, that to anyone with a friendly attitude to humanity it is painful to think that the great majority of mortals will never be able to rise above this view of life"

Sigmund Freud

"Religion prevents our children from having a rational education; religion prevents us from removing the fundamental causes of war; religion prevents us from teaching the ethic of scientific cooperation in place of the old fierce doctrines of sin and punishment. It is possible that mankind is on the threshold of a golden *age; but, if so, it will be necessary first to slay the dragon that guards the door, and this dragon is religion"*

Bertrand Russell

Religion has penetrated every aspect of the society in which we live. From education to politics it has split communities all around the world and has had a strikingly poisonous effect in my own land. It is not even that the religions are that different from each other in this country, the vast majority of both sides are Christian. They have the same God, same Saviour, but still there are fervent hatreds between them. Who are this God and saviour? Did either side even stop to think about what it's about? Some take much advice from the older book while others prefer the newest release.

    The New Testament is supposed to chronicle the life of Jesus, but Christians cannot forget the God of the Old Testament as this is supposed to be the one in the same God. This God, who apparently must have arose through some form of 'spontaneous creation', created the world in 6 days and was so beat that he then needed a day off to recover.

    He created the first man Adam, and then the first women Eve, from Adam's rib (although earlier in Genesis both male and female were created together). He also created all the animals and allowed Adam to name them. He placed the couple in the Garden of Eden and they were allowed to eat of the trees except one, a special tree, the tree of knowledge of good and evil. Apparently, a snake with a mastery of their language talked Eve into this terrible deed, who then convinced Adam to partake, which infuriated God.

Adam and Eve now realised they were naked and fashioned some fig leaves to cover themselves. As Eve was the main culprit, God decided that woman would then have terrible pain and anguish during childbirth, and that man should rule over women. God was not completely unreasonable and made some clothes for them before he ousted them from the garden.

Even in my own experience there are many, many, people who believe this story. Here and now in the 21st century, and working in scientific professions, they actually believe it to be literally true! Robert Green Ingersoll said (way back in 1884 by the way), "if you find any man who believes it, strike his forehead and you will hear an echo. Something is for rent".

The Bible is not even original in much of its most popular fables. Take everyone's favourite story of the flood and Noah building his ark. There are several flood myths from varying traditions around the world (and very popular in areas that are prone to flooding). The Noah flood myth though is almost an exact copy of a story that was within the *Epic of Gilgamesh*, a poem from ancient Mesopotamia that is one of the oldest surviving texts available.

This poem describes Gilgamesh's long journey to discover the secret of eternal life (more on that later) and in it has a Great Flood narrative. This Great Flood was a global flood, caused by the Gods due to the wickedness of man. But there was a righteous man called Utnapishtim, who was ordered to build an ark to save his family, a few others, and all the animal species of the world. Utnapishtim released birds toward the end of the flood to find land, with the boat then finding its final resting place on a mountain. Sound familiar?

Now it would not take a genius to know that the Genesis account for the origin of life is absolute nonsense but religion has an extraordinary power of turning off ones critical thinking. Written obviously by a man, as it was all the women's fault that things went tits up (causing the whole problem of original sin), and that men, would then have the word of God to fall back on to keep their women in line. The nonsense did not stop there, oh no, there was plenty more to come from these ignorant, mystery authors of the Old Testament.

If their plan was to invent the most disturbing, crazy, genocide loving maniac ever created, they achieved their goal. Just read it, any of it and it will be clear to anyone with a modicum of intellect that it's complete drivel; whether you read it as literal or figurative (or any way you like); it serves no purpose to you and is void of either substance or value.

The human race has managed to progress despite religion. This progress is due to many men and women working tirelessly and because of the discoveries of science like the ones mentioned in the previous chapters. Everything being used today has, in some shape or form been altered by those discoveries. It was the answers to the "we don't know" questions that have shaped the world around us. A common answer by theists to a "we don't know" question is, "God did it." There would have been plenty of apologists throughout history who would not have wanted the answers to be found; so they could continue to say "God did it."

I loved both science and my faith and never really consciously thought of any contradiction between the two. Science had the answers to the physical world, while God was the answer to any of *my* emotional, moral and spiritual problems. This was almost to be my undoing.

Even in my pre-pubescent days I wondered a lot about what was my purpose, why I was here, and what path I was supposed to take in life. I prayed and thought about God and wanted Him to guide me through my life. Going through a catholic education we were subjected to at least one daily prayer at the start of the school day. As you are probably aware Catholics bless themselves before and after prayers by making the sign of the cross. As early as 8/9 years old I would not bless myself at the end of the prayers so that the prayer was not to me 'formally complete'. This was (in my mind) to have God with me continually throughout the day to help me be a good person. Religion had got me from the word go; hook, line and sinker!

In fact it had got me so bad I had thoughts of joining the priesthood (this was until puberty, when the lure of the opposite sex dashed any hopes of that). I continued to be a firm believer throughout my teens, twenties, and even into my early thirties, but things were not straight forward during this time period. The questions of 'why' and specifically 'what' I was supposed to *be* kept raising their heads. I felt lost and confused with no answers being provided no matter how much I asked.

Severe bouts of depression and heavy binge drinking were also adding to the problem. How could a loving God who apparently controls everything allow such internal misery? Why could The All Powerful not release me from this suffering? I had seen doctors and psychologists, been put on medication but this did not seem to make any difference. My own gullibility, superstitions and beliefs hindered my ability to face the problem head on and find true answers.

I thought then that God wanted me to get mentally tough on my own. That this was somehow part of his plan to make me into the person I was supposed to be. But I was failing at it and that made me feel even worse. Another possibility (that could only be concocted in the most superstitious brain) was that there was some internal 'bad spirit' causing the problem. I really cringe at the thought of this now but it shows how religion and superstition can screw-up a view of the world. I was led to believe that faith would sort it, and to pray and hope. All the while I was having frequent suicidal ideations, almost constantly thinking about death (and what that meant) and living a life of internal turmoil. The tumultuous cycle continued.

My faith at this point was starting to slip. For someone who would never question his beliefs it was extremely tough for me to become the 'doubting Thomas' (It's pretty clear to me now why that particular story was so prominent in our religious education). I wanted to find some truth, some answers. I wanted information about faith, religion, and Christianity and came across fantastic debates and information online. To be honest, due to my own human bias and yearning for a caregiver, I was actually looking for information that would ground me back into faith - information that would dispel my worries and settle me back into belief.

Some of the debates I watched were between Christians and atheists but unfortunately for 'Team Christianity' young earth creationists were on that side. I mean people such as 'The Banana Man' Ray Comfort, Ken Hamm and Kent Hovind looked so absolutely ridiculous trying to argue a young earth despite all the evidence to the contrary. I could see, for at least the most part that they seemed sincere in what they believed and were convinced the earth is less than 10,000 years old. Also that the story in Genesis of a 6 day creation is literally true (with Adam and Eve and the talking snake) and that Noah squeezed all those animals on a boat while there was a worldwide flood. I thought what planet are these people on and how could they be so unbelievably stupid? But I then took a look at myself.

I, being a catholic, accepted that evolution was true but that God started it all and gave us a conscience somewhere along our evolutionary pathway (weak story I know but it stopped it interfering with my faith. If the catholic dogma had not accepted evolution I would have it banished from my life years ago). I was also supposed to believe in God as the creator of heaven and earth. That he had a son Jesus magically born of a virgin, was crucified, died for our sins, descended into hell but rose again 3 days later and is now happily in heaven beside his dad. That he was due back sometime in the future to 'judge the living and the dead', however that might be done, and that we all could have 'life everlasting', whatever problem that may solve.

These are to name but just a few of the beliefs I was supposed to hold. I realised that people would be looking at me with the same disdain that I had for the creationists, and rightly so. Something really didn't seem right and I needed to find out more. I realised that I never really thought about it properly. The idea of ever questioning my faith had never really entered my mind; I mean never! I took it that it must be true and I was just not trying hard enough to get a strong connection with Him. I was full of guilt and fear. I was subscribing to a world view that sacrificed my intellectual integrity and was making me commit philosophical suicide.

Take the saviour in this Christian worldview; Jesus Christ. His lunatic father that drowned everyone in the world bar one family, ordered genocide, and was not quite bothered about slavery, now had a massive change of heart! He wanted to sacrifice his son (who was also him) so as to save the people of the world from their 'sins'. Is it just me or did he just make a real bollocks of the whole thing – especially for an all knowing all powerful 'God'?

When coming from a position of accepting evolution (which is fact so it doesn't matter if you accept facts or not – they're still true) the timing doesn't quite make any sense either. As I've said 'we' in our current *Homo Sapien* form have been around for approx 200,000 thousand years. This means that God sat back with arms folded and watched for 198,000 years as most of our species struggled and died in their 20's, invariably from simple things like their teeth, infection, or in child birth. He then suddenly decided that now was the right time to send a saviour! Not to send this saviour to an educated population, but to send him to the most backward, superstitious populace available - located in the Middle East.

I believed this man was born of a virgin, died on the cross *and* rose again. This to me then made him an exceptional human, and he must be the son of God. Until I learned that these particular 'qualities', along with others, just made him like several other 'saviours', that have been created throughout history. There are numerous books and essays on these 'saviours' but here are just few from *Listverse*:

Dionysis – Born of a virgin on the 25th of December as a Holy child and was placed in a manger. Was a travelling teacher who performed miracles. Turned water into wine. Known as 'King of Kings', and 'Only Begotten Son'. He also rose from the dead and his 'body' is eaten in a Eucharistic ritual for fecundity and purification.

Krishna – Born without a sexual union. Was visited at birth by wise men and shepards who were guided by a star. Cured several diseases, including a leper. Cast out demons and raised the dead. He celebrated a 'last supper' was crucified and resurrected.

Zoroaster – Born of a virgin and baptized in a river beginning his ministry at the age of 30 but amazed people with his knowledge when he was a child. He cast out demons and restored sight to the blind. He was the 'Word made Flesh' and his followers expected a second coming.

Horus – Born of a virgin and the only begotten son of the God Osiris. Birth heralded by a star. The ancient Egyptians paraded a child and manger in the streets around the winter solstice. There is no data about his life between the age of 12 and 30 similar to Jesus. He was baptised at the age of thirty. Baptiser was beheaded. Walked on water, cast out demons, healed the sick, restored sight to the blind. Was crucified, descended into Hell; resurrected after three days.

And there are others with very similar back stories and life events. This is not a coincidence. In Joseph Campbell's *The Hero with a Thousand Faces* he discusses his 'theory of the journey of the archetypal hero found in world mythologies'. The hero's journey usually involves a number of stages like starting out in the 'ordinary world'; he 'receives a call to enter a world of strange powers and events'; if he accepts the call he then must face 'tasks and trials', often alone; and in its most intense the hero must 'survive a severe challenge'; if the hero returns he can use a 'gift' received from his trials to 'improve the world'. Jesus is nothing more than another mythological 'hero' and this lends credence to Christ myth theorists such as the New Testament scholar Richard Carrier.

The so called 'gospels' were actually written, by who we don't know, decades after this particular 'hero' was supposed to be around doing his thing. Another American New Testament scholar Bart D Ehrman, has the more widely accepted view that there was a preacher named Jesus (one of many at the time), but that the stories in the gospels are unreliable, filled with discrepancies and that Jesus was in no way 'Divine'.

The critical thinking, reason, logic (i.e. virtue) shown by the naturalists, atheists, agnostics, humanists, whatever you want to call them, just made sense. I remember vividly the moment the penny finally dropped. Something just switched in my brain and I said to myself, "holy shit, everything I thought I understood about the world was wrong, there is actually no God, and certainly no reason to believe there was one."

The happiness I felt was so great I laughed out loud for several minutes. Most of the laughter was due to the fact that it took me so long, because instantly, it seemed so obvious. I no longer had to try and justify to myself why the world was in the fucked up state it was, and how God could let it be that way. I no longer expected any 'Divine' help in my affairs and realised it was up to me and only me. The greatest realisation for me was that I owned my own mind. My thoughts and feeling were known to no-one but myself. It's not that I was trying to get rid of God but that I wanted to understand myself and the world around me. "The truth shall set you free" and it did for me. All I had to do was think and as Ernest Hemmingway said "All thinking men are atheists".

Before I finally freed myself from belief I had lost so much faith in the Catholic Church that it was no longer a factor. The God I believed in then was a personal God. A God separate from the church but still a big part of my daily thoughts. I suppose, if people were honest, this is the type of God they have. Someone to talk to in times of need, and personal troubles - but this still removes personal responsibility. Thinking there is still some controlling power in our lives that is looking after us, caring for us, protecting us is, to the individual, similarly psychologically detrimental as any organised delusion.

When I say to myself there is no God, it's an existentialist, naturalist atheistic view of the world. Emmett F. Fields sums it up well;

"Atheism is more than just the knowledge that gods do not exist, and that religion is either a mistake or a fraud. Atheism is an attitude, a frame of mind that looks at the world objectively, fearlessly, always trying to understand all things as part of nature".

Just be aware of another bastardised form of belief that was strewn across the internet and popular TV programming. The so called 'Law of Attraction' and the massively popular book *The Secret*. The simple but mind numbingly dense idea behind this sort of new age pseudoscience is that if you want something bad enough ask the universe for it, and the universe with conspire to get what you desire. If you will hard enough and focus strongly enough on what you want, it will be provided for you. As the Scottish philosopher David Hume said "The life of a man is of no greater importance to the universe than that of an oyster", or as I have mentioned earlier from Johnny B Truant – *The universe doesn't give a flying fuck about you*!

This feeling of some unseen agent interfering in life is one of the human brains biases of over reading determination. This, along with many other factors, fools us into and keeps us trapped within belief. If one is to truly be free, and ultimately *own oneself*, it is up to the individual to 'rise above' these childish, wishful ways of thinking. There was no Garden of Eden, no Adam or Eve, no flood, no Moses, no Exodus, no commandments, and some could argue – no Jesus. There are no miracles and your prayers are not 'answered'. Prayer is simply a way for one to think they are doing something, while in fact they actually do nothing!

People will say they have witnessed miracles but to reply to this I will turn again to the Scottish philosopher David Hume who said "When any one tells me, that he saw a dead man restored to life (or any miracle for that matter), I immediately consider with myself, whether it be more probable, that this person should either deceive or be deceived, or that the fact, which he relates, should really have happened." So if you think you saw a miracle, or worse still heard from someone else that they witnessed a miracle, which is more likely; that indeed a miracle did happen, or you or they are mistaken?

As for prayer, there has been one proper empirical assessment of prayer performed at Harvard, the greatest of its kind. This study showed that patients who underwent by-pass surgery and were prayed for had no statistical improvement in post op complications compared to patients who did not receive intercessionary prayer. In fact the patients who *knew* they were being prayed for did statistically worse!

Chapter 4

'Blind' Faith

"Is man merely a mistake of Gods? Or God merely a mistake of man"

Friedrich Nietzsche

"Your heart's desire is to be told some mystery. The mystery is that there is no mystery."

Cormac McCarthy

"It is hard to free fools from the chains they revere"

Voltaire

There have been a thousand Gods throughout history and every believer is an atheist to 999 of them. So what makes them believe that theirs is the 'true' God? Would it not be more rational to think that *all* are false including the *one* they believe in? People would rather believe in ancient myth than learn the *facts*. Ecclesiastical authority has no credibility on *factual* matters, so why would their authority on any other matters be relevant? All religions claim that their revelations are true but they are all inconsistent with each other, which essentially means to the objective individual, that they are *all* false. Now I am not attacking anybody personally; I am attacking beliefs, or ideas, and the ancient claims made in 'holy' books.

When I was able to stand back and look objectively at the concept of faith it was blatantly obvious, in a remarkably short period of time, that it was both nonsensical and irrational. As a thinking adult, I asked myself a few simple questions about it, and it was ripped to pieces. Why did it take so long to come to this realization? Why did I accept something that was so "patently infantile"? How could I have been so gullible so as to immerse myself in faith and prayer? There had to be a reason why almost everybody I know, and am surrounded by, "will never be able to rise above this view of life." Science again proved to be the source of knowledge I was looking for.

One theory is the by-product theory of religion. There are plenty of books and resources online that tackle this subject but there is one book that succinctly analyses the how's and why's the human mind generates religious belief; *Why We Believe in God(s) – A Concise Guide to the Science of Faith*. Written by J. Anderson Thompson, Jr., MD and Clare Aukofer.

In the book they describe how 'Religion utilizes and piggybacks onto everyday social-thought processes, adaptive psychological mechanisms that evolved to help us negotiate our relationships with other people, to detect agency and intent, and to generate a sense of safety.' And that 'if you understand the psychology of craving fast food… you can fully comprehend the psychology of religion.'

It was vital for our ancient ancestors' survival that they found meat and ripe fruit. It provided a food source high in protein and calories and they ate more than they needed due to the 'unpredictability of food availability'. The brain rewarded our ancestors by releasing brain chemicals that made them feel intense pleasure when eating such foods, and so they craved them. The craving for these essential foods helped our ancestors to work harder to find them and improved their physical state and chance of survival. It is the same pleasure we feel when eating fast foods and sweets and this is a *by-product* of evolutionary adaptations that is now doing us harm.

We have a 'myriad of survival based mental capacities' that 'were indispensible for our survival' and 'these adaptations are the building blocks of religious belief' writes Dr Thompson.

The **attachment system** is the first that really stood out to me. It is the bond between parent and child. When we were young, helpless and at times frightened, we latched onto our parent(s). The bond is extremely strong but it does not stop as we get older but instead drives us to find attachment to a caregiver even as adults. What better caregiver than an all powerful, all loving God in the heavens that will hear our prayers protect and guide us in this life and have a place for us in the next?

We have such a yearning and want to believe in someone/something loving and eternal that this makes the rejection of religion very complicated to our minds. As the French existentialist philosopher Jean Paul Sartre states, "That God does not exist, I cannot deny, that my whole being cries out for God I cannot forget."

Another fantastic ability we have as humans is **decoupled cognition** and it is vital to religious belief. Decoupled cognition is the ability to have a 'complex interaction with unseen others'. We do it all the time, like remembering an altercation, or planning to talk to someone about an issue. We go to the places in our minds, no matter if in the past or the future, and are immersed in that situation. This is a natural ability and in believers it can be used to create a complex relationship with the unseen caregiver God mentioned above.

Closely related to this says Dr Thompson, is **theory-of-mind mechanisms**. It is our 'innate ability to 'read' what another person may think, believe, desire, or intend, in remarkable detail and with remarkable accuracy, and make assumptions based on that'. We can imagine this caregiver God and 'read' what he is thinking (especially about us). We decide what to do to make this God happy and he will continue to help us out, but also we can imagine what he is thinking about us if we behave badly!

Hyperactive agency detection device (HADD) is an extremely interesting concept mentioned by Dr Thompson in his book. It comes up frequently when trying to search for the root of religious belief. (Dr Michael Shermer of Skeptic Magazine talks about it on a couple of interesting YouTube videos). Think of our ancient ancestors in the wild walking through brush or a forest for example. They hear a noise close by. They now have two options; it was the wind blowing, or it was a predator (maybe human) hunting them down. If they think it was the wind blowing but it was a predator, they become lunch and leave the gene pool. If they think it was a predator and it was just the wind then they survive. The predator is an intentional agent and the wind is inanimate.

Of our ancestors, the ones more likely to survive were the ones that gave intentional agency to something inanimate, something unseen. This then makes us, the descendants of those hunter gathers, quick to 'assume the presence of unseen beings and to believe that such beings can influence our lives'. Couple this with the above mechanisms and it's easy to see why one would believe a caregiver 'desires to interact with us' even though it remains unseen and is... well... imaginary.

There are many more fantastic ideas mentioned by Dr Thompson but I want to touch on one more, which I mentioned at the end of the previous chapter - **overreading determination**. I really like this one because I hear comments that are blatant examples of it on a day to day basis. It is our bias toward seeing purpose and design in everything, even though there is none. "The traffic is bad because I'm late." "If I had taken my umbrella it wouldn't have rained." If I had a pound for every time I heard the expression "everything happens for a reason" - no it bloody does not! If you think the universe is on your side (attracting good things toward you for a reason and because you want it bad enough) then it will be easy for you to see things that way because children, and indeed adults, show **promiscuous teleology**.

Promiscuous teleology is seeing and understanding the world and the things within it in terms of purpose. "The world is here for humans to live on" "The grass is for animals to eat" "Trees are for birds to nest in" and so on. This then comes down to us reading situations in the same way. "I didn't get the job because it just wasn't the right one for me." Or a very popular expression here is, "if it's for you it'll not pass you" meaning that there is a reason, a purpose, or maybe an unseen controller not wanting you to get the job because He has something better for you in the future. Sorry to tell you but you didn't get the job because someone interviewed better than you.

Another really interesting ability of humans similar to overreading determination is that of **apophenia**, or what Michael Shermer calls 'patternicity'. It is the 'unmotivated seeing of connections' accompanied by a 'specific experience of an abnormal meaningfulness'. In other words we find meaning in patterns that are completely random. Think of the virgin Mary in a burnt slice of toast, figures in the clouds, hearing voices in random sounds, or seeing a face in the only object in the night sky big enough to give us a pattern! This apparent pattern, or more importantly meaningfulness, that is seen, heard or indeed experienced, can then be attributed to an invisible agent – God.

Apart from the aforementioned self deception involved in religious belief, there are other factors that play a huge role. Obviously the fact of indoctrination at a very young age is going to have a significant impact on the chances of following a theistic world view. The people doing the indoctrination are authority figures such as parents, teachers and clergy. The people, which children know and trust, with whom they have a special bond. The child simply thinks they must be telling the truth and they must know what they're talking about. This is deference to authority and it can undermine an individual's assessment of themselves and the beliefs they hold.

I would rather 'defer' to theories and ideas that go through the most stringent testing (scientific method) and come from the most intelligent people on the planet. I think it is reasonable to 'believe' the geniuses of our time that skeptically assess their work rather than to 'believe' the most deluded individual on the planet 2000 years ago.

I mentioned it earlier about the 'doubting Thomas' story that he didn't believe Jesus had risen from the dead and wanted to see the bodily evidence of the crucifixion. He was made out to be such a terrible individual for not believing. I had some small doubts a few times throughout my life but I quickly banished them to the back of my mind because I did not want to become 'the doubter'.

The story of Christianity had two main protagonists as far as I was concerned. One, which was explained to us as the trinity of the father, the son and the Holy Ghost, and the other was Satan, evil, bad spirits whatever you want to call it. That there was some sort of battle between these two sides for the control of the hearts and minds of man. This was another huge reason for not doubting, because it meant that the bad side was working its way into and winning the battle in the psyche. That this evil force might penetrate so deep as to somehow curse the individual for life. Not only this life but to then have to spend eternity in hell in the next! If that's what was going to happen rest assured any terrified young boy or girl would be quick to dispel any, even minute, inkling of doubt.

There are of course the tribal factors and the feelings of being part of something bigger than you - a sense of safety and comfort with being part of this extended family that gathered together every week to sing a few tunes and say a few prayers. It felt comforting, sitting quietly thinking about life and was about the only time during the week that I sat down quietly with my family.

Religion in this way is part of a system of anchorings, inherited firmaments that are essentially a form of distraction from the truth of reality - the inevitable truth that we are going to die

DEATH

The act of dying; the end of life; the total and permanent cessation of all the vital functions of an organism.

Chapter 5

And To Dust You Shall Return

"Man is literally split in two: he has an awareness of his own splendid uniqueness in that he sticks out of nature with a towering majesty, and yet he goes back into the ground a few feet in order to blindly and dumbly rot and disappear forever"

Ernest Becker

"We are no more than a breathing piece of defecating meat, destined to die and ultimately no more important than a lizard or a potato"

Sheldon Soloman

We have evolved cognitive abilities much greater than any other species that ever walked on this planet. It is precisely because of these abilities that we are able to recognise and contemplate our own deaths.

Tom Stoppard writes in *Rosencrantz and Guildenstern Are Dead*, 'Whatever became of the moment when one first knew about death? There must have been one, a moment, in childhood when it first occurred to you that you don't go on forever. It must have been shattering – stamped into one's memory. And yet I can't remember it. It never occurred to me at all. What does one make of that? We must be born with an intuition of mortality. Before we know the words for it, before we know that there are words, out we come, bloodied and squalling with the knowledge that for all the compasses in the world, there's only one direction, and time is its only measure'.

Animals have the fight or flight response to danger, as do *we*. However they only have that fear in the present moment and choose in that moment to use the rush of hormones to either fight or evade the danger. We have the ability, as mentioned in the previous chapter, to decouple our cognition. "We can anticipate and imagine future dangers but the physiology is the same and the body can't tell the difference between the past and the future." This leaves us carrying a huge burden of anxiety about our own death that would cripple us if not controlled.

It's not that this realisation of our eventual demise at a time and place we don't even know is *a* problem - it's because it is *the* problem. The classic essay *The Last Messiah* written by Peter Wessel Zapffe in 1933 starts 'One night in long bygone times, man awoke and *saw himself.* He saw that he was naked under cosmos, homeless in his own body. All things dissolved before his testing thought, wonder above wonder, horror above horror unfolded in his mind.'

'Whatever happened? A breach in the very unity of life, a biological paradox, an abomination, an absurdity, an exaggeration of disastrous nature. Life had overshot its target, blowing itself apart. A species had been armed too heavily... a menace to its own well being. Thus it is thought, for instance' writes Zapffe 'that certain deer in paleontological times succumbed as they acquired overly-heavy horns. The mutations must be considered blind, they work, are thrown forth, without any contact of interest with their environment.... In depressive states, the mind may be seen in the image of such an antler, in all its fantastic splendour pinning its bearer to the ground.'

He describes that the only way one can continue is to repress the realisation of this meaninglessness existence and eventual death. He addresses four major kinds of repression 'naturally occurring in every possible combination.' These are; isolation, anchoring, distraction and sublimation. **Isolation** is 'a fully arbitrary dismissal from consciousness of all disturbing and destructive thought and feeling.' He describes **anchoring** as 'a fixation of points within, or construction of walls around, the liquid fray of consciousness. Though typically unconscious, it may also be fully conscious (one 'adopts a goal').' He continues, 'Any culture is a great, rounded system of anchorings, built on fundamental firmaments.... (God, the Church, the State, morality, fate, the law of life, the people, the future).... the basic cultural ideas.'

The third mode of protection is **distraction** were 'one limits attention to the critical bounds by constantly enthralling it with impressions.' I'm sure the reader would recognise this as a popular technique, as would I, when jumping from one thing to the next with intense focus but when the focus subsides despair can quickly set in and another distraction is needed urgently before complete mental collapse.

The fourth and last protection against panic and despair is **sublimation**. He describes it as 'a matter of transformation rather than repression.' As an artist I can fully understand this remedy. Painting is a way for me to transform the internal pain and suffering into a 'valuable experience' and use my 'positive impulses' to 'engage the evil' and put it to my own end.

Another way in which we tackle the paradox of a desire to live and death is the idea of immortality. One does not have to worry about death because it's only a transition into another eternal life and it is one reason (if not the biggest) why religion is so fundamentally important to believers.

In Stephen Caves TED talk he describes the four ways of gaining everlasting life; things might vary slightly from culture to culture, but these are the four ways that best describe our attempts at achieving immortality. The first is the **elixir** of life. The idea of a potion that when drank will provide the individual with everlasting life, or eternal youth. Alchemists in various ages and cultures sought the means to formulating the elixir of life.

The second is **bodily resurrection**, as with the central character of Christianity. That when the time comes one would rise up to the heavens, in their current form, to continue their eternal life with the Creator. Now both of these, even to an irrational person in the 21st century are completely absurd.

The most popular concept to get around the problem of death is that of mind/body dualism (and is why I will spend slightly more time on it). That yes, the human body is made of matter and atoms, but that the 'spirit' or 'soul' or 'consciousness' is made of different 'stuff', and it is this 'stuff' that somehow travels to somewhere where we will exist as us, in an afterlife. It is natural to look at a living person and a dead person and conclude that the dead person is missing something; that something is life. It's not that something has 'left' them and gone somewhere else; it's like extinguishing a candle, the flame doesn't go anywhere, there is just no longer a flame.

Your mind, your body it's all you. They are not two separate entities that somehow dislodge from each other when you die. Your mind is a *process* produced by the function of the brain and once the brain dies the process can no longer be produced. In science it is no longer even an interesting subject of debate because we now know, due to our understanding of physics that this is not possible, and that, no question about it - there is **no** life after death.

The last way described in the talk to achieve at least symbolic immortality, is that of one's legacy. Yes, we can die but our legacy can live on, well after we are gone. It explains a great deal about our modern culture and the almost universal desire for fame and fortune (although other reasons are present) so that one would make such an enduring mark on society that it would out-last our mortal existence.

More recently scientists have inquired about our existential dilemma with empirical investigation and have posited what is described as the **terror management theory** (**TMT**). The documentary film, *Flight From Death – The Quest for Immortality*, is about TMT. TMT is derived from cultural anthropologist Ernest Becker's 1973 Pulitzer Prize-winning work *The Denial of Death*, and elaborated upon by scholars such as Sheldon Soloman, Tom Pyszczynski, Jeff Greenberg and Holly McGregor.

Becker says "The idea of death, the fear of it, haunts the human animal like nothing else; it is a mainspring of human activity – activity designed largely to avoid the fatality of death, to overcome it by denying in some way that it is the final destiny of man."

In other words;

The fear and terror about death creates such anxiety in humans that *everything* we do, and have done, whether consciously or subconsciously, is as a result of this anxiety.

Becker termed the overwhelming feelings of terror as 'annihilation anxiety' saying it was vital for people to manage this anxiety to function. There are two main ways in which we defend ourselves against this terror and that is our **culture/worldview**, defined as 'a set of beliefs about the nature of reality shared by groups of individuals that provide meaning, order, permanence, stability, and the promise of (as mentioned above) literal and/or symbolic immortality to those who live up to the standards of value set by the worldview.' The other is **self-esteem**, defined as 'one's belief regarding how well one is living up to the standards of value prescribed by the worldview.'

Ones worldview is then bonded with deeply rooted existential fears. This causes people, when they have an increased awareness of death, to vehemently defend their cultural beliefs and vigorously try to meet the standards of their culture so as to increase their self-esteem. Not only this but people then have much less tolerance for, and anger toward, members of other cultures. In other words if I wanted to start a war in another country or against another culture, I would just make the public much more aware of death i.e. increase their mortality salience using the media and they would be much more likely to consent to aggressive action. This is a hypothetical scenario of course!

It explains why different cultures throughout history have such trouble co-existing peacefully. The idea of immortality is so tied into one's worldview, whether that is literally as in religion, or symbolically as in national pride, that an attack of any kind against one's worldview is an attack against one's very existence. That has made the average person conform, accept, and in cases enthusiastically applaud the most heinous crimes ever committed against humanity.

Culture including religious belief, is nothing more than a 'shared fabrication of reality' to provide meaning and security in an unsure world.

Culture is an illusion, religion is a delusion. They have separated humankind into groups, destined to fight and kill one another. Moreover, the individuals' acquirement of self-esteem, the very thing that makes us happy as it protects us from the 'annihilation anxiety', has become based on that illusion.

But what if every member of the human species accepted truth through empirical evidence, and progressed with a shared goal of improving the living standards of *all* members of our species? This will not happen not anytime soon because cognitive dissonance plays its role and people will concoct any excuse to try to question evidence that contradicts their worldview (e.g. even saying the speed of light is not constant!).

We do not have to be part of any worldview that needs us to 'believe' anything. If science proves that something didn't happen or that it was impossible that it did happen then it didn't happen (talking snake, virgin birth, resurrection, flood etc, etc). Extraordinary claims require extraordinary evidence. The evidence simply does not exist for *any* of the extraordinary claims made by religious groups. There are *no* miracles. We can think for ourselves in every aspect of our lives. We don't need to be told anything or to obey any rules regarding behaviour. If something is wrong, then it is wrong no-matter what the situation, or who the perpetrator is. The virtues of acceptance and truthfulness are ultimately important so why take part in the charade of 'faith'?

You can get your self-esteem from within. Know at the end of the day, that you have done your best to help others, tried your utmost to improve as a human being and faced any problems as best you could. Of course we make plenty of mistakes but it's only a mistake if you did not learn from it.

I nearly committed the biggest mistake any human could make – take my own life. I now feel, with hindsight, that I understand the true, deep reason, why I wanted to do it. My anxiety was annihilation anxiety, or to put it another way, deep existential angst. Not knowing when death was going to come, feeling my existence was meaningless. There was one way of solving the problem of having the fear of death, not knowing when it was going to happen and living a meaningless life - to actually control or end these feelings – commit suicide. I now understand some ways to protect myself against the anxiety through improved self-esteem and acceptance of death.

If we all could accept death as part of nature and accept that we are "risen apes, not fallen angels". Accept that we as humans have to take responsibility for our thoughts as well as our actions. Being human is an ever-evolving path through life and most of us are being dragged, beaten, pushed and kicked through life by our emotions. By allowing this we are limiting, if not completely destroying, our ability to have what each of us should strive to have - a happy and fulfilling life.

HAPPINESS

State of well-being characterized by emotions ranging from contentment to intense joy.

Chapter 6

The Holy Grail

"The happiness of your life depends upon the quality of your thoughts: therefore, guard accordingly, and take care that you entertain no notions unsuitable to virtue and reasonable nature"

Marcus Aurelius

"There are more things to alarm us than to harm us, and we suffer more often in apprehension than reality."

Seneca

The dictionary simply describes happiness as; 'the state of being happy'. Sounds fairly simple doesn't it? However when you are unhappy it feels like the most difficult thing in the world to find. Moreover, at times of true unhappiness it feels like one is destined to be that way forever. That one's life will be an endless void, a black hole, a never ending pit of despair that out of which one seems unable to climb.

Philosophers throughout the ages have pondered the question of happiness. From Plato and Aristotle, to de Montaigne and Schopenhauer, they have tried to understand the nature and attainment of happiness. The problem in our society and our modern culture is that people confuse wealth with happiness. I too fell into the trap. Reading books about how to make money, like *Rich Dad, Poor Dad*, and others like *The Secret* (mentioned earlier which would almost convince you that all you had to do was to 'think' yourself rich). This *is* what most people think they want and need - to be rich.

I'll put it this way: Imagine having loads of money, living in a huge house with a Ferrari parked out front; but feeling empty, depressed and unfulfilled. Now imagine having enough money for you and your family and that you are all happy. That you also get to do something that inspires you and spend more time with people you love. As Epicurus put it, "It is better for you to be free of fear lying upon a pallet, than to have a golden couch and a rich table and be full of trouble."

The two philosophers that have had a large impact on my idea of happiness are Epicurus and Aristotle. (The overall philosophy for living without sadness I dedicate a whole chapter to later)

Epicurus (341-270 BC) was an ancient Greek philosopher and founder of the school of philosophy called Epicureanism. The purpose of philosophy for Epicurus was to live a happy, tranquil life. This would be achieved by *ataraxia* – peace and freedom from fear. And also *aponia* – the absence of pain.

He thought that pleasure and pain were at the centre of human morality and that they were so important to human existence that all actions were governed by seeking pleasure and avoiding pain. He felt that one of the most important aspects of being happy was to be around friends but also spend time alone, in quiet reflection. He taught that moderation and only the necessary things (food, shelter, friendship, self control) were needed to be happy. Unnecessary (external) things were not needed for happiness such as some crave in today's society like excessive wealth and fame.

Two areas that stand out for me in Epicurean philosophy are the attitude to the gods (people were polytheists at that time), and the attitude to death. Epicurus taught that the gods were already in a state of bliss and were not bothered about human affairs – "If God listened to the prayers of men, all men would quickly perish; for they are forever praying for evil against one another." Another quote attributed to Epicurus about

God(s), and has been popular among atheists for centuries is;

> "Is God willing to prevent evil, but not able? Then he is not omnipotent.
> Is he able, but not willing? Then he is malevolent.
> Is he both able and willing? Then whence cometh evil?
> Is he neither able nor willing? Then why call him God?"

His attitude to death (remember this was over 2200 years ago!) was that death does not concern us. When we are alive death does not yet exist, and when we are dead we cannot experience anything – so no more worry about death!

> "Why should I fear death?
> **If I am, then death is not.**
> **If Death is, then I am not.**
> Why should I fear that which can only exist when I do not?
> Long time men lay oppressed with slavish fear.
> Religious tyranny did domineer.
> At length the mighty one of Greece
> Began to assent the liberty of man."

Aristotle (384-322 BC) was a Greek philosopher and scientist and is one of the greatest thinkers in the history of western science and philosophy. He presented his theory of happiness or *eudaimonia*, in his work *Nicomachean Ethics*.

Aristotle saw happiness as the ultimate purpose of human existence. His theories suggest that we desire things as we believe these things will make us happy, while happiness is always an end in itself.

For Aristotle happiness could not be gained or lost within a few minutes, or days, but more to do with how well one has lived up to their full potential until this point in time. To exercise the human power of reason, to develop character, and the acquirement of virtues or excellence at being human – this *is* happiness!

Virtue is the point between a deficiency and an excess of a trait, not a mathematical mean but a 'golden mean' between two opposite extremes. It is not just splitting the difference but sometimes closer to one extreme than the other: "at the right times, about the right things, towards the right people, for the right end, and in the right way, is the intermediate and best condition, and this is proper to virtue." Take the virtue of courage for example. It lies in the middle of the spectrum between foolhardiness and cowardice (vices). Temperance (virtue) lies between self-indulgence and insensibility. Pride (virtue) lies between undue humility and excessive vanity.

The Latin maxim dictates- *in medio stat virtus* – In the Centre Lies Virtue. The reason I choose it for the title is twofold: I wanted to bring the idea of virtue to the forefront of people's minds and show that it indeed lies in the middle. Much more importantly, I feel it is exactly the *lack of virtue* that is at the centre of most people's unhappiness.

If we behaved with virtue and acquired wisdom and knowledge about ourselves; showed courage and diligence in the face of fears and obstacles; acceptance in the light of facts; practiced temperance and discipline in our indulgences; took responsibility and accountability for ourselves and our actions - life would be much less painful.

Happiness then has three ingredients which I have come to see as more dominant than any others. I have come across them in philosophy, books, websites, and online blogs and in my own life, they are these:

1) Happiness is a state of mind. In other words, what you tell yourself about the situation you're in (your perception) and how you control your emotions about the situation decides whether you are happy or not. Don't see any situation as 'bad'. Use it to show virtue or your flexibility and ability to change and adapt. Be happy no matter the situation. This takes time to learn and control but will give you ***power***.

2) Knowing, and owning you. Be free! Find out what makes *you* tick and work at that. Know what drives and motivates *you* to achieve. Ignore any external influences (parents, society, money etc) and concentrate on *you*. This takes effort and a lot of meditating over one's own true desires and needs in this life – this is how you find ***meaning***.

3) Working at something that truly inspires you. When you are completely immersed in such an activity gives a huge sense of purpose, **_pleasure_** and fulfilment. Find or create it now.

The experience of this type of work is *'flow'*, and was coined by Hungarian psychologist Mihaly Csikszentmihalyi, who wrote a book of the same name. If this activity also has the added element of helping others then your inner satisfaction and feeling of pleasure will increase exponentially. You will truly be at peace while performing this work. Its then, and only then, that you will be realising your potential, which in itself will be to the good of society. Happiness is therefore a continual process of mastering oneself, and one's abilities, with a goal of achieving one's full potential. Performing activities for they own sake rather than any ulterior motives.

The film *The Pursuit of Happiness* gets its title from Thomas Jefferson's writing within America's Declaration of Independence. It is terribly misleading. To insinuate that happiness is some sort of destination is quite frankly wrong. It implies that if you work hard enough, struggle and fight your way through hardships, that someday you will be happy. In fact the complete opposite is true. These 'struggles' and 'hardships' are obstacles that shape who we are, and what in fact, define us. As Marcus Aurelius states in his *Meditations*; 'The impediment to action advances action, what stands in the way becomes the way.'

Do not focus on being happy or wealthy. Focus on finding or creating your niche and working with your unique abilities. You do not have to reinvent the wheel to be unique but just to put your twist on something that already exists. Focus on what's real and virtuous, within the bounds of nature. If someone should show you that what you thought was true were in fact wrong then be glad of finding the truth for it is this that you seek. You then have the truth, and can live with a self assurance that what you are doing is true and virtuous - at that moment. Another moment in the future might be different but you don't have to give it, or any other moment apart from the one you're in, a second thought. For it is in this, the *present* moment, that happiness is found.

There is a well known saying that "every cloud has a silver lining". This insinuates that you wanted something but didn't get it and that there will be some small amount of, fairly insignificant, good to come out of the disappointment. I've heard it so many times! But you don't have to see the cloud as disappointment at all. The cloud is *just* a cloud. It will not hurt or harm you, and is not disappointment unless you tell yourself it is a disappointment.

Much more importantly the silver lining is the surprise! It is the unexpected thing you didn't see coming, a development that puts you on a path to something new. And I tell you the surprise is always much better than what you wanted before the 'cloud' seemingly formed. Like in Douglas Adams' *The Long Dark Tea-Time of the Soul;* 'I may not have gone where I intended to go, but I think I have ended up where I needed to be.'

Bring to an end the fear of the unknown, or the fear of 'failure'. For it is in the unknown that we grow. Failure does not exist unless it is you who say it. Stop procrastinating, stop worrying, stop thinking whatever it is that you want to do will 'fail'. There is only one true failure – not trying in the first place. I assure you each time you try you will learn something and increase your will and resolve for the next attempt. As Mark Twain puts it; "Twenty years from now you will be more disappointed by the things that you didn't do than by the ones you did do. So throw off the bowlines. Sail away from the safe harbor. Catch the trade winds in your sails. Explore. Dream. Discover."

If you face an obstacle, the courage, ingenuity and determination you conjure will strengthen your character. Other than helping others, overcoming obstacles is the greatest of feelings one can possibly enjoy. It took Thomas Edison, the American inventor 10,000 attempts to create the light bulb but he said "I have not failed. I've just found 10,000 ways it won't work." He also said, "Just because something doesn't do what you planned it to do, doesn't mean it's useless"

How does one learn to control emotions? Why do we have a purpose at all? I can throw all the fancy quotes I want at you, I can give you inspiration through the written word but if you do not understand the *thing* it is you're trying to control and what *drives* it, you're seriously limiting your chances of personal happiness.

Chapter 7

Taking Control

"Human nature is complex. Even if we do have inclinations toward violence, we also have inclination to empathy, to cooperation, to self-control"

Steven Pinker

"Remember, it is not enough to be hit or insulted to be harmed, you must believe that you are being harmed. If someone succeeds in provoking you, realise your mind is complicit in the provocation. Which is why it is essential that we not respond impulsively to impressions; take a moment before reacting, and you will find it easier to maintain control"

Epictetus

Sigmund Freud was an Austrian neurologist and the founder of psychoanalysis. He created a whole new approach to the understanding of the human personality and it is his theory of the Id, Ego and Super Ego that will help you understand both how you behave and how others behave toward you. Before we go any further, forget the idea of someone having a 'big ego', or being 'egotistical' as this will confuse you and have little to do with psychoanalytical theory. Also, that particular ego, as we commonly refer to it, is huge barrier to happiness!

Freud postulated that the human personality/psyche is made up of three parts which are not physical parts and not quite distinct from each other. There is a great deal of actions and reactions between all three which also travels throughout the conscious, preconscious and subconscious; also defence mechanisms are employed by the psyche. For the purposes of simplicity and understanding, I will try and just give the very basics.

The Id is the instinctive section of personality that develops first and demands immediate satisfaction regardless of any consequences. It is the part involving our sex drive and anger and seeks out pleasure. When we deny it this immediate satisfaction it makes us feel pain or displeasure. It resides deep within the subconscious and works on the *pleasure principle*. Think of a baby crying to be fed or when it's tired, or of someone getting angry or aggressive when they did not get their way. That's the Id!

The Ego is the decision making part of the personality and tries to satisfy the needs of the Id while also trying to adhere to social norms and follow the rules of society. The Ego is the rational, problem solving part of the brain and it works on the *reality principle*.

The Super Ego is what most people would consider to be their 'conscience' and is also where the most of our 'Ideal self' or 'Higher self' resides. The Super Ego punishes the Ego with feelings of guilt and self loathing if it cannot control the powerful Id. It will also punish you if you are not adhering to the standards/or the *needs* of the 'Higher self'. The Super Ego can also reward us through the ideal self when we behave 'properly' by making us feel proud.

A great metaphor for gathering all three parts together and seeing the kind of activity going on in the mind is this:

The **Ego** is a man standing on a chariot.

The **Id** is a crazed group of horses pulling the chariot.

The **Super Ego** is the man's father sitting behind him criticising his actions when he cannot control the horses.

No wonder we feel a bit crazy at times! These three parts are battling within us continuously. There is ongoing battling between the Id and Super Ego for supremacy while the poor Ego, you, is stuck in the middle.

When I was going through therapy a couple of years ago I had no idea about and we didn't discuss, the Id, Ego and Super Ego. What we did discuss was how I had reacted to various situations that I found myself in between therapy sessions. If I reacted emotionally, impulsively or irrationally that was the Id and I was behaving like a *child*. If I was overly self critical, continually 'beating myself up' over certain decisions, that was the Super Ego and I was behaving like a *critical parent*. If I was rational, logical, and studied what was going on and came to a reasonable conclusion, that was the Ego and I behaved like an *adult*.

This is very helpful and once you recognise which part of your psyche is trying to react in certain situations, you can at least have some sense of what is going on and *choose* to act like an adult, *through* the Ego (with a little bit of help from the Super Ego). If you don't, it's you who suffers. Remember, you want to keep your suffering to an absolute minimum. Freud said "the Ego is not the master in his own house" - but to be happy, you might have to make it so.

When people are acting up around you, you can then just *observe* their words and actions. If they are overly critical toward you and maybe asking too much of you or not being an adult, it's not *them*. That is to say, don't take it personally, just stay calm. Observe (don't even really take it in) what they are saying and if needs be, respond, as an adult. If you let your Id in, it will cause a fight! If you let your Super Ego in, you will believe the crap they say and 'beat yourself up' for the rest of the day, week or maybe much longer.

This works the same when they are overly aggressive or maybe even just slightly antagonistic toward you. Remember it's not *them*, in this case is *their* Id. The same rules apply. Just *observe* their words, have no stake in what they say and keep your self control by staying within the ego. A fight, be that verbal or physical, could easily ensue in this scenario but you are above these animalistic, barbaric, cavemen practices. Anyway if you were to take part in some 'fisty-cuffs', you will only punish yourself later for losing control (even if you did kick his ass). Like Bohdi Sanders says in *Warrior Wisdom: Ageless Wisdom for the Modern Warrior*; 'Never respond to an angry person with a fiery comeback, even if he deserves it...Don't allow his anger to become your anger.'

Your mind may try and get you to apologise and cower down to the aggressor but this too is not befitting of a man in control. Stay adult, stay logical, stay rational, and remember to act with virtue and speak the truth. They have just lost their own control - that's all. You don't have to lose yours.

Marcus Aurelius at the start of book 2 in his *Meditations* talks about the above scenarios. Although 2000 years ago he did not have the psychoanalytical structure of the Id, Ego and Super Ego the premise of neutrality is the same:

'Say to yourself first thing in the morning: today I shall meet people who are meddling, ungrateful, aggressive, treacherous, malicious, unsocial. All this has afflicted them through their ignorance of true good and evil. I have seen that the nature of good is what is right, and the nature of evil what is wrong; and I have reflected that the nature of the offender himself is akin to my own – not a kinship of blood or seed, but a sharing in the same mind, the same fragment of divinity. Therefore I cannot be harmed by any of them, as none will infect me with their wrong. Nor can I be angry with my kinsman or hate him. We were born for cooperation, like feet, like hands, like eyelids, like the rows of upper and lower teeth. So to work in opposition to one another is against nature: and anger or rejection is opposition.'

More recently Dr Steve Peters a consultant psychiatrist has written the book *The Chimp Paradox*, which tackles this same underlying Id - the animal instinct - or as he calls it, our inner chimp. His theories have been a massive influence in the improved performance of numerous elite athletes. His ideas of how the mind and emotions work, can help anyone manage their minds and become the person they would like to be. He breaks the mind down into a similar structure as Freud but with some differences: The Id is your 'inner chimp'; the Ego is 'human' or you; and the Super Ego is your 'guiding moon' or the computer that is the reference point that the human and chimp must go through before they act. He gives an excellent insight into how to manage your chimp and see it as separate from you. Importantly, he also writes about creating a 'Stone of Life' or a set of reference values and beliefs that brings everything into perspective and helps manage your critical self (Super Ego).

What if some criticism you are receiving is justified? What if the individual in front of you is talking rationally from their Ego? How would you even know? Well we all know partially innately (nature) partially due to nurture, what is right and good behaviour. If both parties are being rational and you were in the wrong then you must still continue to stay within your Ego. Be an adult and accept responsibility for your actions - it was probably acting out the Id's demands that caused the fault (even if only slight). But, and a big BUT, don't let the Super Ego launch in and 'beat you up'. It was a mistake, learn, forgive (yourself) and forget.

I have included the Id, Ego and Super Ego in the 'Happiness' section for very good reason. If you do not learn to control your mind and take responsibility for your actions (that ultimately come from the mind) you will give yourself far more grief than needs be. It doesn't do your or anyone's happiness any favours going round in 'Id Mode', letting your chimp run wild, grumping when you don't get your way or being aggressive to others. Dr Peters calls this an '**Alpha Wolf Mindset**'. Avoid going round in 'Super Ego Mode' too – i.e. being self sacrificing, taking no responsibility on and being overly obedient; especially to people not worthy of your obedience. Dr Peters calls this the '**Snow White Mindset**'.

Learn to avoid these practices and be wary that you can impulsively jump into them. Take a moment and choose the Ego, choose to be adult, choose to be human. As Lao Tzu said, "He who controls others may be powerful, but he who has mastered himself is mightier still".

Apart from genetics a lot of things will have happened to us growing up to shape our minds. These things can leave us with a powerful Id, making us now, at this moment, hyper-emotional, insecure or irrational. Things, people, situations, could have also increased the power of the Super Ego, causing us to carry round the proverbial 'big stick' to beat ourselves with at every opportunity. Start *now* with a clean slate. Recalibrate your Id and Super Ego to neutral. From here on out you are in control. They both still have the ability to jump in suddenly, at any opportunity but you will recognise them as *separate* from the real you. You will learn, in time, to use them to your advantage!

As a slight aside to 'self control' I would say to not be controlled by other people's thinking. Don't let what you think other people are thinking have an impact on your choices in life. Otherwise the choices, to all intents and purposes, are not yours. In David Dieda's *The Way of the Superior Man* he writes, 'Live as though your father were dead.' Sounds pretty blunt doesn't it. But it makes a great point. You cannot live your life trying to please other people or live up to what you think *their* expectations are, especially *your perceived* expectations of your father or mother, or both. If they reared you right and true they should then expect you to be a man, or women, that will choose his/her own destiny and fulfil his/her own needs and desires. And especially, don't be controlled by delusions of what you think an imagined deity may be thinking either!

There are a lot of *ifs* regarding self control. Rudyard Kipling put them beautifully into a single poem - If:

> *If you can keep your head when all about you*
> *Are losing theirs and blaming it on you,*
> *If you can trust yourself when all men doubt you,*
> *But make allowance for their doubting too;*
> *If you can wait and not be tired by waiting,*
> *Or being lied about, don't deal in lies,*
> *Or being hated, don't give way to hating,*
> *And yet don't look too good, nor talk too wise:*
>
> *If you can dream—and not make dreams your master;*
> *If you can think—and not make thoughts your aim;*
> *If you can meet with Triumph and Disaster*
> *And treat those two impostors just the same;*
> *If you can bear to hear the truth you've spoken*
> *Twisted by knaves to make a trap for fools,*
> *Or watch the things you gave your life to, broken,*
> *And stoop and build 'em up with worn-out tools:*
>
> *If you can make one heap of all your winnings*
> *And risk it on one turn of pitch-and-toss,*
> *And lose, and start again at your beginnings*
> *And never breathe a word about your loss;*
> *If you can force your heart and nerve and sinew*

To serve your turn long after they are gone,
And so hold on when there is nothing in you
Except the Will which says to them: "Hold on!"

If you can talk with crowds and keep your virtue,
Or walk with Kings—nor lose the common touch,
If neither foes nor loving friends can hurt you,
If all men count with you, but none too much;
If you can fill the unforgiving minute
With sixty seconds' worth of distance run,
Yours is the Earth and everything that's in it,
And—which is more—you'll be a Man, my son.

Chapter 8

Our Driving Forces

"Our animal origins are constantly lurking behind, even if they are filtered through complicated social evolution"

Richard Dawkins

"If you plan on being anything less than you are capable of being, you will probably be unhappy all the days of your life"

Abraham Maslow

"A musician must make music, an artist must paint, a poet must write, if he is to be ultimately at peace with himself"

Abraham Maslow

We are social animals who have a long evolutionary past through various different species. Both of these facts have a major impact on what our needs and desires are. We have obviously an underlying need to eat, sleep and reproduce etc but being social we have a desire for respect, status, love and acceptance.

There is an interesting area of study called the evolutionary psychology (EP) of consumption. Gad Saad is an evolutionary behavioural scientist that works in this area and has published the book, among others, called *The Consuming Instinct*. It uses Darwinian principles to describe an ultimate cause for the products we buy and the services we use in modern society. In other words our consumption today is linked to the needs we had to reproduce and survive etc, in the very distant past.

The four key Darwinian modules are: survival, reproduction, kin selection and reciprocal altruism. I mentioned about the consumption of fatty burgers (in religion section) as an adaptation of our need for high calorific food in an environment where food would have been scarce. That's an example of the survival module at work.

The kin selection module shows that when we buy gifts for our kin, a perfect pattern emerges as to the amount we spend on them. The more closely related we are genetically, the more we spend. This is not a surprise and in the past kin selection would have given an increased chance of at least some of the individuals DNA surviving, by giving preference to siblings, children etc.

Reciprocal altruism is kind of 'you scratch my back I'll scratch yours' although the person doing the 'scratching' would have to incur some sort of cost. This would have been important among our groups of ancestors to help with bonding and increase the chance of the 'receiver' helping the 'giver' out on a future occasion. This is where the phenomenon of gift giving comes from.

Reproduction (or mating) would obviously have played a major role with the groups of our ancient relatives - otherwise how would we be here! The EP theory would suggest that we purchase things and behave in a certain way, for instance, for sexual signalling or status improvement. Women wear high heels and men buy fancy cars for similar sexual signalling purposes.

Interestingly enough, the reason men find high heels attractive is due to the fact it creates lordosis in the women wearing them. The heels raise the buttocks of the woman by roughly a 30 degree angle, which is a more sexually receptive position usually taken when they are about to mate. This is sexual signalling and a visual preference intoxicating to men that finds its origins far back in our evolutionary past.

Men buying fancy cars is a type of 'peacocking' to show females that they have status and would be a good mating choice. Not only this, but it has been empirically tested to show that men when driving a car in an area with onlookers, have testosterone spikes in a fancy car (it was a Porsche) but nothing in an older, 'lesser' car.

These are wonderful examples of how our 'lowly origins' shape our behaviour today, in the modern world. All of us going about our daily business with deep, subconscious, animalistic forces at work – and we don't have a clue that they have a huge affect on what we do. The social structure in our past species would have also been much more animalistic but our desires or needs would have been pretty much the same. We would have lived in much smaller groups with an 'alpha male' type hierarchical system within the groups.

It was vital for us to rise within the group to achieve status and respect and with it, the most food and opportunity to reproduce. To accomplish this we would have gained valuable social information by learning from or mimicking the dominant male or dominant members within the group. In the documentary *Starsuckers* they talk about an experiment performed with rhesus monkeys to show the 'power' the dominant male has over the lower tier monkeys.

The experiment had a monkey sit in front of two screens. The monkey got rewarded with juice when it looked at one screen and not the other. He sacrificed this 'reward' and looked at the second screen on only two occasions; when it showed the hind quarters of a female (no surprise there!) and when it showed a picture of the dominant male.

This watching and learning about the 'dominant male' or who is 'successful' and 'influential' is hardwired into us through our evolutionary past to increase our chances of survival. We need to not only learn how to be superior within a group, but more importantly what not to do. This means for us today in a global, media and advertising bombarded culture, it is the people who they show on screen as successful and influential we are trying to 'mimic'. We learn from them how to behave socially or how not to behave in most cases. The how *not to* behave is more important social information than how to behave and it is why we are drawn to scandal rather than positive stories.

There is an 'illusion of intimacy' in our brains with regard to what we see on T.V. and other media. The part of the brain involved cannot tell the difference between T.V. and reality. Most of us are probably not even aware that it has an effect on us. This is because this type of hardwired mechanism lies deep within the subconscious.

We are powerfully and naturally attracted to fame because we think it brings happiness in its wake, through money or perceived "success". We have these huge expectations of what our lives should be like but the odds are stacked heavily against anyone getting to be super-rich *or* famous. Why do you think celebrities endorse absolutely everything and charge mini fortunes to do it? Because people want what celebrities wear, eat, drink or use and the products or services they sell. This is hardwired phenomena of social learning from millions of years of evolution from which it is difficult to escape.

People spend money they don't have on things they don't need, trying to fill a social void. They foolishly think they are 'learning' from these 'celebrities' how to climb the social ladder to apparent 'happiness'. This approach to improve 'status', self-esteem, self-respect and fulfilment is doomed to fail. As the philosopher Seneca said; "It is not the man who has too little that is poor, but the one who hankers after more." The type of capitalist society we live in depends on 'creating' needs and depends on this 'hankering' to increase consumer consumption. The products *are not* in the vast majority of cases to improve the individuals' life or lessen their needs - it's simply for profit.

Self esteem is no trivial matter and as I have mentioned previously, is our 'buffer', or protection against annihilation anxiety. Self esteem lies within **Maslow's hierarchy of needs**. This is a theory in psychology proposed by Abraham Maslow in 1943 and elaborated upon later in 1954. It is not a scientific or empirical assessment of needs but more of a humanistic approach to what motivates us. He gathered together the information concerning human needs by studying people who he thought were exemplary. People such as Einstein, Jane Addams, Eleanor Roosevelt and Fredrick Douglas.

Originally only having five groups of needs, starting with the most basic fundamental needs at the bottom, he then later added a sixth. These six needs for humans to fulfil their true potential were (starting from the most basic); physiological needs, safety needs, love/belongingness needs, esteem needs, self actualisation and the pinnacle that is self transcendence (also seen in

Cloningers temperament and character inventory). Below is the hierarchy of needs as it is usually presented in a triangle.

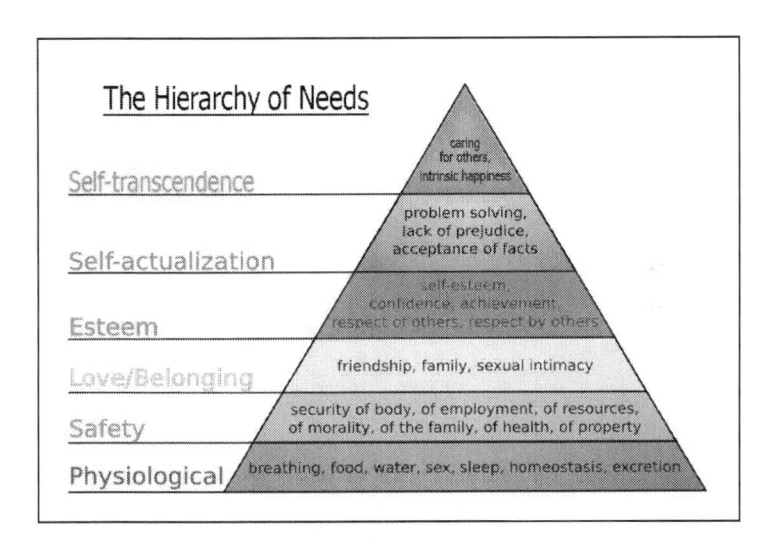

The Hierarchy of Needs

- Self-transcendence — caring for others, intrinsic happiness
- Self-actualization — problem solving, lack of prejudice, acceptance of facts
- Esteem — self-esteem, confidence, achievement, respect of others, respect by others
- Love/Belonging — friendship, family, sexual intimacy
- Safety — security of body, of employment, of resources, of morality, of the family, of health, of property
- Physiological — breathing, food, water, sex, sleep, homeostasis, excretion

Physiological - Fairly self explanatory and would be similar to most living animals on this planet. Without any of these needs we simply would not be alive.

Safety – We want to feel safe and secure in our environment. We want to know the resources to fulfil our physiological needs are available to us. We want to have steady employment and with it, financial safety.

Love/Belonging – We want to have friends and family and also a need for sexual intimacy with someone who love us. This is different from the sex need in the basic physiological section.

Esteem – Self esteem is vitally important and is built on several key areas such as; confidence in ourselves, a sense of achievement in our everyday lives, a need for beauty or aesthetically pleasing surroundings and possessions, respect for others, Maslow included here a feeling that we are respected by others but I would argue that if you respect yourself while progressing to the next stage/stages, what others think of you will not affect you in any way.

Up until this point within the progression we are just coping with life - merely surviving. We are just about happy enough with being comfortable and having a few luxuries. We will have an empty, low level of 'happiness' that would not feel truly fulfilling but at least not depressed. To truly achieve fulfilment in life you must move on to the higher levels using *self direction*.

Self-actualisation – Acceptance of facts is a very significant aspect of self actualisation and it's what the first half of this book is all about. Others aspects are; creativity (not just artistic), spontaneity, problem solving, discovery of self and knowledge of the world and contribution to your society - remember that your 'society' is over 7 billion people strong!

Self-transcendence – The pinnacle of any human existence. Forget money or fame, this is what you are aiming for along with self-actualisation. With self-transcendence you will feel enlightened (or an intrinsic feeling of happiness), feel a need to help others and see the much, much bigger picture (which I have also tried to show in the earliest parts of this book).

It is every human being's ultimate goal to achieve self-actualisation and self-transcendence but it is obvious that any path to this will not happen if there are huge holes in the more fundamental areas. If you are struggling to find food and water you will not be too bothered about finding your higher self! If you don't feel safe and secure in your life, be that with a threat of violence, not enough money to pay the bills or worried that you might lose your home, transcendence might be the last thing on your mind.

These 'holes' will need to be filled in before any progression could be possible in the true sense. These 'holes' may even be self manufactured. For example, worrying and fear created though a lack of vision or self control. Where are the 'holes' within *your* needs? Are they imaginary? Are you just coping instead of living? Find the answers to these questions through your own personal self discovery.

There are people that transcend themselves (by way of a short cut) by giving their lives to others. Such as hospital staff or people in war torn areas and members of religious groups. The main point is that self transcendence should be *self directed* (Mihaly Csikszentmihalyi calls this 'intrinsic motivation') a choice, a deep inner yearning coming from within the individual, without feeling 'forced' by external events or internal delusions. The individual must know the huge role played by cognitive bias and cognitive dissonance in the choices they make. They know that 'material success' is not success at all.

Do not squander the potential that lies within you. Raise your awareness of *self* and the world within which you reside. Once you raise your awareness, it is then that you will cultivate your skills and ultimately create your own *passion*. We are all individuals and have individual qualities unique to each other.

Find your unique qualities by working hard (really, really hard) in the things you like doing *and* experience things you never experienced before (you may like those more than you anticipated) – it's no more complicated than that. When you are trying new things do them with boldness and confidence and without hesitation, otherwise it's not a real attempt. Find out what you like spending time doing, and spend more time doing it.

I use the word 'passion' because there are probably things you are 'passionate' about in life already. Cultivation of a passion or passions *is* working on your purpose! It is only when you are passionate about something that you will be fit to work hard enough and give it everything you have (the power and energy for this comes from the Id), to become a *master* at it.

Ask yourself this:

If you had all the <u>money</u>, and all the <u>time</u> in the world, what would you do?

You could be a working at it already but be distracted by the materialistic consumerist culture we have making you not even realise. Are you doing what you want or love to do? If you are helping others while not sacrificing virtue – it's quite possible that you are already where you need to be.

      You could be self-actualising already. If you are not then why stay in the 'rat race' working at something that almost sucks the life out of you. We have a limited time on this planet that could end at any second. This life is not a preliminary, not a warm up for the main show – this life is the only show. Use that realisation to take a chance and make an attempt to be the person you desire to be.

      I was so overtaken by my own fears and anxieties, my own lack of self-worth that I was not even aware that my passions were right in front of me; I love gaining new knowledge, I love sharing that knowledge with others, I love helping others, I love painting abstracts as a way of self discovery, I love to create, I'm starting to love writing, I love science, I love music, I love art, I love meeting new people.

Lying watching TV all night may feel like the easy thing to do (your chimp mind will even tell you to do it) buts it's not fulfilling. It's not a productive activity for an intelligent, sentient being. A bigger TV, fancier clothes, and the newest smart phone - these things are nice to have surely but they are not what your life should be about. They do not define you and if they were not part of your life you would not be any less happy.

What gave me the clarity of thought, the drive to work hard, the courage to say what I feel, a new child-like enthusiasm for life, an increased social awareness, the release of my fear of death and anxiety about life? It was a philosophy, a *new way of thinking* that encompasses many virtues. This philosophy was new to me but goes way back over 2000 years - this philosophy is STOICISM.

Chapter 9

Be More Stoic

"For what prevents us from saying that the happy life is to have a mind that is free, lofty, fearless and steadfast - a mind that is placed beyond the reach of fear, beyond the reach of desire, that counts virtue the only good, baseness the only evil, and all else but a worthless mass of things, which come and go without increasing or diminishing the highest good, and neither subtract any part from the happy life nor add any part to it?

A man thus grounded must, whether he wills or not, necessarily be attended by constant cheerfulness and a joy that is deep and issues from deep within, since he finds delight in his own resources, and desires no joys greater than his inner joys." Seneca

Stoicism was a philosophy founded by Zeno of Citium in the early 3rd century BC. They presented their philosophy as **a way of life in accordance with nature**. They maintained that man should not be controlled by his emotions but rather that man should control his emotions and desires to be free from suffering. Stoicism was a thriving way of life until the Emperor Justinian I banned its practice as pagan and at odds with the doctrine of Christianity (not before they took/stole stoic ideas and incorporated them into Christianity).

They taught that mans **reasoning** abilities (our greatest quality) about life and the situations he found himself in, were at the forefront of reducing suffering. That there were things in our control such as emotions and reactions and we can choose to give assent or dissent to these emotions. That there were also things out of our control and we should not give any time or energy to these things.

They believed in the **Logos** or 'Gods'; a 'universal principle which animates and rules the world' and universe. This was not a personal God that should be invoked by any individual (I see it as the universe and the laws of physics which control it). They taught that a life lived using rational thought and reasoning was **virtuous**. Pleasure should not be sought but to live by virtuous principle is the goal and duty in life. The four cardinal virtues of a stoic (from Plato) are; **wisdom, courage, justice** and **temperance.** They taught us to see things as they are (in accordance with nature) and not as we wanted them to be.

<u>The stoic definition on Google is:</u>
A person who can endure pain or hardship without showing their feelings or complaining.

<u>The urban dictionary is slightly more accurate and is this:</u>
Someone who does not give a shit about the stupid things in this world that most people care so much about. Stoics do have emotions, but only for the things in this world that really matter. They are the most real people alive.

<u>One definition that best sums up stoicism is from Nassim Nicholas Taleb:</u>
"A Stoic is someone who transforms fear into prudence, pain into transformation, mistakes into initiation, and desire into undertaking"

They taught that nothing was inherently good or evil but, as it was put by Epictetus, "Men are disturbed, not by things, but by the principles and notions which they form concerning things." I acquired three books from original stoic philosophers; *Meditations* by Marcus Aurelius, *Discourses and Selected Writings* by Epictetus, and *Letters from a Stoic* by Seneca.

Stoicism has completely transformed my life. I used to worry about everything!; myself, my health, what people (everybody) thought of me, money, status, my reputation, material goods, *any* decisions, what 'God' thought of me, my addictions, my clothes, my car, my parenting skills, how good I was as a husband, father and son, my work, the list could go on and on. I am now free from this worry and have an inner calm and the power of mind to feel unconquerable (I am aware that this can change).

I feel it is *my duty* to try and share what I have learned with as many people as possible. I want to try and show that there is the power inside each one of us to be virtuous in our day to day lives (no matter what that day entails; there is no reason not to be virtuous in your deeds).

My introduction to stoicism was in all respects accidental, or more appropriately, natural. I was searching on YouTube for ways of improving my financial situation, as I thought *it* was the root cause of my worries. But I found a channel called 'Fight Mediocrity – Big Ideas for a Better Life' created by a young man called Malkhaz Geldiashvili. Malkhaz is 'dedicated to helping people find the courage to do what they are passionate about' and his videos are fantastic (When I first started watching his videos he had about 30,000 subscribers. Watching another of his videos today and he now has nearly 300,000).

He takes what is normally a quite mundane area of self help and self improvement and turns it into something much more interesting and enjoyable. He does short animated videos that highlight the important points within books and makes them relevant to everyday life. It was his video of Marcus Aurelius' *Meditations* (along with others) that started me on my new path in life (There are similar channels such as Optimize Your Journey and Super

Charged that use animation to show the fantastic ideas and knowledge that can be found in books).

He showed that books were not pointless and that they held invaluable information to improving one's life. Another book review that I viewed much later was that of *The Obstacle is the Way* by Ryan Holiday. It describes how icons of history used the principles of stoicism to overcome adversity and to achieve greatness in their respective fields. The subtitle of the book is 'The Timeless Art of Turning Trials into Triumph'. A fantastic read and has inspiring stories throughout.

Every person can use stoic ideas to improve their lives and live a happy life through virtue, reasoning, fortitude, courage, wisdom, inner calm and clear judgement. I've tried to put together a few of the points I found most useful from the philosophy that had the biggest impact on diminishing my anxiety and depression to *almost* nil.

People have **unrealistic expectations** from being overly optimistic. We dream about a fantastically rich and prosperous future and when things don't seem to be going our way we get down and depressed about it. We don't need to expect anything. What actually arises will invariably be somewhat different from any expectations good or bad, that we may have conjured. You can also treat what happens with indifference and so not get angry or suffer in any way. After a while you will not think about the future or expect anything from it.

"Anyone who likes may make things easier for himself by viewing them with equanimity." Seneca

"Wealth is the slave of a wise man. The master of a fool." Seneca

---

See that **emotions come from within**. If you are feeling like shit it is because you are *choosing* to feel like shit. Practice self control. Whether you believe it or not you can control your emotions (choose ego). Think rationally and you will see that what is causing the problem is likely to be either outside of your control (and therefore nothing to get upset about), or you're allowing it to affect your mind in a negative way. If you have done your best at something but it appears to 'fail' this is also no reason to get upset because you have done your best, and that's all you can do. Remember you do control what you do. You can decide to take action to start building self-esteem.

"You have power over your mind - not outside events. Realize this, and you will find strength." Marcus Aurelius

"He suffers more than necessary, who suffers before it is necessary." Seneca

---

What's holding you back? What are your **obstacles**? If there are things that you need to do but are too afraid to do them, do them anyway, find a way. You will feel better and learn more in trying than you ever will in not even giving it a damn good try. (See Ryan Holidays book, *The Obstacle is the Way*)

"The impediment to action advances action, what stands in the way becomes the way" Marcus Aurelius

"It is not death that a man should fear, but he should fear never beginning to live." Marcus Aurelius

---

Increase your **wisdom** and don't be wilfully ignorant of yourself and society. To burst the proverbial 'bubble' that surrounds you and see past your own front door to the rest of the world. This takes time and effort but is extremely fulfilling. It will bring a lot of 'perceived' problems into proper perspective and allow you to give them the assent or dissent they deserve.

"No man was ever wise by chance" Seneca

"Timendi causa est nescire -
Ignorance is the cause of fear." Seneca

Be **brutally honest** with yourself and your 'beliefs'. See the world for what it is, not as you would have it. Enjoy the wonderful things that science has brought us. Be aware of the list of biases (about the length of your arm) that we are susceptible to, such as; the Dunning-Kruger effect, confirmation bias etc.

"If someone is able to show me that what I think or do is not right, I will happily change, for I seek the truth, by which no one was ever truly harmed. It is the person who continues in his self-deception and ignorance who is harmed." Marcus Aurelius

"And see that you keep a cheerful demeanour, and retain your independence of outside help and the peace which others can give. Your duty is to stand straight – not (to be) held straight." Marcus Aurelius

---

Concerning this materialist world of **possessions**. These have no bearing in and show nothing of one's true character. If you would like them and can afford them, that's fine. Don't put yourself into debt (causing anxiety) for 'things' that are not part of self actualisation or transcendence.

"enjoy them without pride or apology either, so no routine acceptance of their presence or regret in their absence" Marcus Aurelius

---

Happiness is found in your duties and not in the results of these duties. You do not control the results and therefore should not be concerning yourself with them. Enjoy what you're doing, if it is virtuous. Give yourself, all your attention, to the task at hand and believe you are doing right.

"Do every act of your life as though it were the very last act of your life." Marcus Aurelius

Have the "acts of a man with an eye for precisely what needs to be done, not the glory of its doing" Marcus Aurelius

---

You will come across **bad people** at many a time on this journey through life. There is a quote that says 'people are generally good' but my experience has shown that plenty of them are bad and in no way virtuous. Do not let their badness infect you - even if they are members of your own family. You don't owe them anything. It is in their nature to be bad so let them be that way. Continue on with what you have to do and ignore them. Do not be angry at them for doing bad to you as anger is self defeating.

"To pursue the impossible is madness: and it is impossible for bad men not to act in character" Marcus Aurelius

"The best revenge is to be unlike him who performed the injury." Marcus Aurelius

Be **present in the moment** and stop **procrastinating**. Do what needs to be done with virtue and good humour. Use the limited time you have to do well and that time will not be wasted. Remind yourself to be happy *right now*. Not in the future, not tomorrow, nor next week but right now. Epictetus asked himself at the end of each day - what did I do right? What did I do wrong? What duty is left undone?

"No wandering. In every impulse, give what is right: in every thought, stick to what is certain." Epictetus

---

Know that **death** is coming to us all and that death is indeed final but noting to be frightened of. It is simply a part of nature. Our fear of it, as a species, has crippled our ability to progress and created cultures for comfort; but instead created havoc and separated the species more than anything in history.

"Death: There's nothing bad about it at all except the thing that comes before it—the fear of it." Seneca

"Life is never incomplete if it is an honourable one. At whatever point you leave life, if you leave it in the right way, it is whole." Seneca

The difference with the stoics compared to other philosophers was that they knew life was tough and didn't shy away from the fact. To the stoics life could not only be bearable in the face of hardships but that the ability to face these hardships without complaint, defined who you were. They taught not only a philosophy but a *practical* way of looking at life to reduce our suffering and to continue no matter what the circumstances.

The scientific method has taught us the realities of our world by removing biases from our interpretation of that reality. Existentialism discusses the angst felt and the meaninglessness of that reality. Stoicism teaches us how to deal with that reality.

Stoic ideas have filtered down through the centuries and you can see the ideas present in more recent literary works (although it is important to be aware of some of the pseudoscience and woo woo that sometimes engulfs the ideas). There are specifically two books that have underlying stoic principles within them and give a more modern approach to improving your life and your self esteem. These are *The Six Pillars of Self Esteem* by Nathaniel Branden and *The Four Agreements* by Don Miguel Ruiz.

The six pillars of self esteem that Branden describes are:

1. **The practice of living consciously** - How often do we go through our days on auto-pilot not giving anything

proper thought? We need to be more conscious of our thinking and our decisions. We should be present in the moment and consciously decide to do what is best for us.

2. **The practice of self acceptance** – There are many things we cannot change about ourselves or our situation but there are also many things we can. We must accept the things we cannot change so that we can then focus and give energy to the things we *actually can* change. We need to stop wasting our energy and time worrying about what is *not* in our control.

3. **Practice of self responsibility** – We must take charge of our own thoughts and actions because the responsibility is *ours and ours alone*. Simple things such as eating healthy and getting some regular exercise can and does do wonders for our self esteem. There are no potions or pills that will magically change things for us. However, if we accept the responsibility and are willing to put in the hard work, anything is possible.

4. **Practice of self-assertiveness** – We don't need to repress our ideas for fear of being ridiculed but instead should stay true to our ideas and our identity. You may think that people will actually care a lot about what you do but they actually don't. On the contrary, people will respect your self-assertiveness and you will gain respect practicing this pillar.

5. **The practice of living purposefully** – This is closely linked to pillar 2 (self acceptance) because once we accept who you are then it's time to purposefully work at improving the areas we can change. Having and working with purpose is vitally important, not just for self esteem but it also brings meaning to our lives.

6. **The practice of personal integrity** – Think of integrity as the reputation you have toward yourself. To have personal integrity is to adhere to your own *personal* rules and moral code. This is achieved with congruence of your words, thoughts and actions. What you think you must say, what you say you must do – and remember as Albert Camus said, "Integrity has no rules."

I particularly like Ruiz's *The Four Agreements* because they are easy to remember. His agreements are:

1. **Be impeccable with your word** – Our words are powerful and we can use that power to bring people up rather than put them down. No gossiping but only to say what is right.

2. **Don't take anything personally** – People will say and do numerous things to us in our lives but these are outside of our control. Don't take it personally and it will not have an effect on your self-esteem.

3. **Stop making assumptions** – How many times are our assumptions wrong? They are probably wrong on most

occasions. If we eliminate making assumptions from our daily though patterns it will greatly reduce our stress and negative thinking.

4. **Always do your best** – Probably the four most important words for reducing regrets and guilt. Our 'best' can vary from day to day but if we do our best, under any circumstances, we cannot fault ourselves nor have a negative opinion of our efforts.

Philosophy and books contain many important lessons and instructions for us in our daily lives. The reason is that the thinkers, or authors, were just ordinary human beings like you and me that had the same struggles and trepidations about life. They were intelligent and eloquent enough to put the lessons on paper and it's up to us to use their experiences to better our own situations – that's the reason they put their ideas on paper!

Chapter 10

Revelations

"The only way to deal with an unfree world is to become so absolutely free that your very existence is an act of rebellion"

Albert Camus

*"In the midst of winter, I found there was, within me, an invincible summer.
And that makes me happy. For it says that no matter how hard the world pushes against me, within me, there's something stronger – something better, pushing right back"*

Albert Camus

We are as free as any bird in the sky, any fish in the ocean, any animal wandering the African plains - *if* we would only let it be so. This freedom is born out of the fact that our existence is indeed an absurdity. Who was to know that on this tiny lump of cosmic rock a thinking species was to evolve? What is *more* absurd is that we, having this freedom, have then made our own shackles and imprisoned ourselves. Shackles made in our attempts to be free from our annihilation anxiety.

We have created mass delusions on a truly epic scale among our species - but there is no reason to do this. These delusions, that we call religion, have been created to give meaning in an 'unsure world' and for the individual to feel part of something bigger than themselves. But as Edgar Allan Poe said, "All religion, my friend, is simply evolved out of fraud, fear, greed, imagination and poetry."

Everything has become an illusion. And illusions are intangible, shallow and destined to fail. The question of suicide was the driving force behind this book and if we are to truly face the problem of suicide then we must face it head on; no nonsense, no pseudoscience, no dogma, no lies, just the truth of the situation and then - right action. The "reassuring fables" are empty and even if they do 'work' for certain individuals, it is still an evasion of the *actual* problem. As Seneca said "It is better to conquer our grief than deceive it" or as Csikszentmihalyi puts it, "religions are only temporarily successful attempts to cope with the lack of meaning in life; they are not permanent answers."

If our mortality salience is high and our self-esteem is low, it is a recipe for disaster – a recipe for suicide. Therefore if we reduce our mortality salience, or its effects, and increase our self-esteem we should have protection against taking our own lives. So knowing that there is such a thing as annihilation anxiety, knowing there are parts of our psyche creating anxiety and fear, knowing the importance of self-esteem and knowing the importance of a meaning or purpose to life - gives us targets to aim at. We possess the power regarding these things and should take *responsibility* and be *accountable* in our efforts.

As I stated at the start of this book, young men are five times more likely to commit suicide than young women. Women appear to be better at utilising the repression techniques described by Zapffe (isolation, anchoring, distraction and sublimation). They seem to hold on to firmaments such as their children or friends better than men and give their life meaning in this way. Indeed, men too are a firmament for women and feel the pressure this creates. Men also do not want to appear 'weak' and will struggle on their own until it's too late instead of seeking help to increase their emotional intelligence. Men also have very decisive all or nothing thinking and choose more brutal, definitive methods in taking their own lives.

From an evolutionary standpoint I think the hardwired social learning that is making us consume, the illusion of intimacy from TV, is also having a detrimental effect on the mental health of young men especially. Men are learning from subtle subconscious signalling what it takes to be 'successful' or the 'dominant male' from celebrities – an almost impossible level to attain. These social signals would lower a man's self-esteem, social esteem and perceived social status leaving him to struggle, feeling isolated, in his own environment. We must try and escape this type of conditioning by thinking bigger, and smaller, at the same time.

We now know that we are "made of stardust" and have in fact become "a way for the universe to get to know itself." We are part of the universe and the universe is part of us. If we have a desire to feel part of something bigger than ourselves, we already are! We are actually a part of everything because everything, including ourselves, is made of atoms created by the cosmos. We then have a choice, to dimly fizzle out throughout our lives like a white dwarf - or own ourselves, own our lives, be unconquerable and be like... a supernova.

To accomplish this and live the greatest life we possibly could live we must address the fear of death. We must accept its inevitability. Accept that it's all going to be over some day. Accept that death is indeed, final. This virtue of willing acceptance should reduce our annihilation anxiety to the point it will no longer cripple us. No longer will we need to hold on to any wishful thinking, delusional firmaments or depend on this illusionary culture. No longer will something bad happen to tip us over the edge, because we are no longer floating near the edge to be tipped over. Moreover, we should use the knowledge of death to our advantage, as Steve Jobs said, "Remembering that you are going to die is the best way I know to avoid the trap of thinking you have something to lose. You are already naked. There is no reason not to follow your heart."

Even if our self-esteem does subside at times you shouldn't feel the same deathly, overwhelming anxiety as before, because you are managing the *actual cause* of the anxiety – our fear of death. If you do, you can use your new found stoicism to control over-reaction, keep things in perspective and put forth proper, objective action. It is the objective action that *creates* self-esteem. Self-esteem is not something mystical that others were lucky enough to get, you have to have action.

Self-esteem was also, in our long distant past, a way of us to gauge how well we were being accepted within our 'group' (as mentioned above). If our self-esteem was low and we were not being accepted there *was* a high likelihood that we would have perished. We would have needed the anxiety to kick us into gear and to work at increasing our acceptance to ensure our survival. We no longer need this acceptance but our brains are hardwired to need self-esteem.

I believe we can now attain this increased self-esteem from our own intrinsic motivations, because the same rules do not apply today as did for our lowly ancestors. We don't need to be accepted to stay alive but we still need self-esteem to reduce our annihilation anxiety, reduce our existential angst, to stop us from wanting to take our own lives.

In the 2014 film *Whiplash*, Miles Tiller plays a gifted and ambitious young jazz drummer who enrols at a prestigious music school in New York. The jazz instructor played by J.K. Simmons is a rude and obnoxious psychopath. He mocks, ridicules and insults the musicians, especially Tiller, to the extreme. But Tiller does not give in, and uses the struggle to dig deeper, push harder, and mouths the words "Fuck you" to Simmons in the climactic scene. He then lets his own instinctive genius shine through in a moment of cinematic awesomeness! Simmons at this moment smiles. He has seen that he did what he needed to do to get the best out of Tiller.

We need to use our problems, our obstacles, our depression, our low self-esteem as a push toward something greater, a push to creating the best *you* there can be. As Ryan Holiday writes, 'It's this all too-common impulse to *complain, defer, and then give up* that holds us back'. 'See it as an opportunity because it is often in that desperate nothing-to-lose state that we are at our most creative.' 'Our best ideas come from there, where obstacles illuminate new options'.

In my darkest days in the past I used to pray and hope and plead to God to please take the pain away. I wanted God to take my life in an accident or through disease so my family wouldn't have to live with the fact their brother or son took his own life. I would think of driving my car off the road at high speed, or into an oncoming lorry, so at least it would not look like suicide - just... an accident.

I now do not regret having that pain at all, in fact, it's quite the opposite. For being at the bottom, in the mental gutter, in complete anguish at times, pushed me to answer the big questions, to read and to learn the reality of this life. My studying philosophy, cosmology, biology, psychology and theology - all came from my anguish. Camus said that "The evil in this world almost always comes from ignorance" - I just tried to make myself *less* ignorant.

I had to stick with it. I had to 'slug it out'. To stick with the boxing analogy I was expecting to swing a 'haymaker' to sort my problems but this usually isn't the way it is. You have to 'stick and move', use your cunning, creativity, perseverance and prepare for the long haul, prepare for setbacks. On numerous occasions I had to roll with the punches and remember it's the 'punch you don't see coming that knocks you out'.

I don't know if the singer Sia knows about annihilation anxiety but she certainly alludes to it in her song 'Bird set free'. She obviously had some very dark days and I can relate to her lyrics in 'Chandelier' in my own struggles with alcohol. 'Bird set free' explains both how it feels when depressed but more importantly the freedom felt when you own yourself, and overcome that obstacle.

She sings:

> *'Clipped wings, I was a broken thing;*
> *Had a voice, had a voice but I could not sing;*

> *You would wind me down; I struggled on the ground.'*

And later;

> *'a scream inside that we all try to hide;*
> *We hold on so tight, but I don't wanna die, no*
> *I don't wanna die, I don't wanna die'.*

But when the freedom is felt;

> *And I don't care if I sing off key*
> *I found myself in my melodies*
> *I sing for love, I sing for me*
> *I shout it out like a bird set free*
> *No I don't care if I sing off key*
> *I found myself in my melodies*
> *I sing for love, I sing for me*
> *I'll shout it out like a bird set free*

Even if you cannot feel the freedom yet, and it may take some time and hard work to get there, comfort yourself with the phrase "this too shall pass" - because it does. Nothing lasts forever - refrain from all or nothing thinking. Even if you have to break time down to minutes, or even seconds to get through the really bad times.

Think: "What can I do to change this, what positive activity can I perform to get me through the next few minutes or seconds?" Not to get through this week, or today - just this moment. It can feel almost impossible to control thoughts at this low ebb (but that can be improved with practice) so just *do something*. Read something, put on a song, clean, have a shower, work at something, exercise. Also use the good times between the lows (when you are thinking more clearly) to prepare yourself for the next one. Tell yourself that these bad feelings may return but you will be ready and waiting with fortitude and courage, not only to overcome them but to use them to your advantage!

It may come that the only way to overcome these feelings is by seeking help. If you had heart disease you would see a cardiologist, if you had a broken leg you would see an orthopaedic surgeon – you have a psychiatric problem and need to see a psychiatrist – there is no shame what-so-ever in seeking their help.

Avoid (if possible) any negative short term distractions such as heavy drinking or drugs etc – you *know* it's only going to make things much worse. It's your own responsibility to change things using objectivity, reason, and virtuous thinking and action.

We are social animals and Aristotle, Epicurus, and now the longest study done on happiness, all point to the ultimate importance of friendships and relationships in being happy. Enjoy other peoples company and confide in people you trust. Share your joys and worries with the people close to you and you will feel their support lift you. Spend more time with the people you love but don't change to get love – you shall be loved for who you are.

Recognise the arbitrary nature of nature and remember you will succeed in some things but not in others. People you love will die, both old and young. Terrible things will happen as well as the good. Things will happen that we have completely no control over. People will be complete assholes. People will let you down. You will be stabbed in the back. There is no rhyme or reason to most things and that's alright – embrace the uncertainty. You don't need to be taking everything to heart and cause yourself undue stress and grief. It's not emotionless to see it this way and you are no less of a person for not getting upset where others expect you should. You are just seeing things as part of nature - we *are* part of nature.

Once you start overcoming your problems don't think you have it all worked out. Don't let some success give you a false sense of security. New obstacles will arise, each one different from its predecessor, requiring new skills and tools to overcome. Rejoice in your fearless approach to the problems and know that no matter how "hard they push; you have always something stronger inside, pushing right back."

You will start to show the world your greatness, your talents, *you*, in all your shining glory. However this comes with a warning: people are, as Nietzsche said, "Human, all too human", and will be bitter, bitchy and envious of you. You must ignore them and remember, as Bernard M. Baruch says, "the ones that matter don't mind, and the ones that mind don't matter."

Observe people when they are not being virtuous to you and never take it personally. Observe yourself too. Study what thoughts you are having and what is driving you. Observe the world around you to see what's actually going on. When you feel, as you should, as a brother or sister of all humans, you will be absolutely appalled with the treatment your fellows are receiving around the world.

Closer to home with our kind of capitalist social and economic structure and consumerism culture, it is the people with the *least* virtue that climb to the top and essentially control and exploit the rest. The greedy, the narcissistic, the wicked, the arrogant, the easily corrupted, these are the people who will rise to positions of power within the capitalist system we have. As John Maynard Keynes puts it; "Capitalism is the astounding belief that the most wickedest of men will do the most wickedest of things for the greatest good of everyone."

The system thrives on our fear (and debt) but the paradox is that this system also allows us the freedom of thought, freedom of speech and freedom of action necessary to flourish. So release your fear, gain self-esteem internally and follow your own life path - "be so absolutely free that your very existence is an act of rebellion."

In the Preface I quoted Albert Camus: "There is but one truly serious philosophical problem, and that is suicide..."

The quote continues... "Judging whether life is or is not worth living amounts to answering the fundamental question of philosophy."

So ***make*** your life worth living and ***make*** a world worth living in.

Be kind, be courageous, be patient, persevere, persist, endure, be honest (with yourself), be vigilant, gain wisdom, be mindful, have integrity, be independent, be creative, be self-aware, show compassion, forgive, be generous, have temperance, and bloody have fun! Most of all, work your ass off at being who *you* are! This is because your existence precedes your essence.

"What is meant here by saying that existence precedes essence? It means first of all, man exists, turns up, appears on the scene, and, only afterwards, defines himself. If man, as the existentialist conceives him, is indefinable, it is because at first he is nothing. Only afterward will he be something, and he himself will have made what he will be." Jean Paul Sartre.

It is therefore your decision; a choice to do activities you will enjoy and become what you decide to be. You cannot choose properly what you desire unless you are still, and listen and then choose. This stillness will be frightening in itself, for it can only be obtained by letting go of everything, by laying yourself bare. All thoughts and superficial external distractions you have been using up to this point to avoid life itself shall be erased, and you will be able to transform yourself through the work you love to do.

There will be fear and a reluctance to attack these choices at the start but this is normal. Once you start the activities you will be provided with internal feedback that will give you a more accurate direction in your work. If you are a bit confused when starting out, think of this from Austin Kleon's book *Steal Like an Artist*: 'Draw the art you want to see, start the business you want to run, play the music you want to hear, write the books you want to read, build the products you want to use – do the work you want to see done'.

If you are in despair, depressed, or indeed suicidal, you will have already realised that all else is meaningless. You have tried to 'fit in', you have tried to be part of the tribe, but it *has not*, and *will not*, satisfy your yearning to express to the world the being that is you. The chaos you are feeling should be welcomed for it will force you to change but more importantly as Nietzsche said; "One must still have chaos in oneself to give birth to a dancing star." The 'chaos' is present because we have no focus and feel helpless; powerless in our own world. The 'dancing star' becomes present because the chaos forces us to separate ourselves from the outside world, to look internally for reward, and cultivates a focused mind for work *we choose* to do.

The fact that you are here now, reading this, shows that you have courage, that you are braver than you think.

So if you want to believe in something; believe in yourself. If you want to have faith in something; have faith in yourself.

All else is madness.

Acknowledgements

This book has only been possible due to the support of my family and a few close friends that helped me share my anxieties and made life bearable enough to continue when I thought it wasn't. I was lost, alone and suffering but special people throughout the years have had a huge influence on me.

Special thanks must be given to my wife Clare who has been with me for 14 years and has put up with far more than anyone should ever have to. Big thanks to my closest brothers Laurence and Eoghan who I can always rely on for a word of encouragement in dark times. To my sister Mary who got me out of many psychological black holes back in my boozing days. To my father who showed me how to be stoic before I knew what stoic was. To MJ, a long time friend and mentor whose influence has shaped much of my life.

The professional help has been vital and the fact that the real road to recovery started with a phone call to Lifeline shows how invaluable it is to have it. Thank you Ruth and Catrina the counsellors that changed a broken man. Thank you to the GP's I've seen over the years also.

Lastly I thank all those free thinkers, philosophers, authors and scientists that have showed the folly of human conceits and were more interested in truth than allowing any of their own biases to shape their reality. A reality that I can now enjoy – most of the time. I still have some dark times but am continuously trying to learn to keep them to a minimum.

Some Further Reading / Viewing (To get started)

Chapter 1 – From Dust

Bryson, Bill. *A Short History of Nearly Everything*. Black Swan, Broadway Books, 2003.

David Christian: The History of Our World in 18 minutes. TED talk. YouTube

Hawking, Stephen. *A Brief History of Time – From the Big Bang to Black Holes*. Transworld Publishers / Batam Press 2011.

Hawking, Stephen and Leonard Mlodinow. *The Grand Design – The Answers to the Ultimate Questions of Life*. Transworld Publishers / Batam Press 2011.

Michio Kaku: The Universe in a Nutshell. Big Think. YouTube

The Best Documentary Ever!! The Story of Earth and Life – The Highable. YouTube.

Chapter 2 – Well I'll be a Monkey's Uncle

Darwin, Charles. *On the Origin of Species* (Oxford World's Classics). Oxford University Press, 2008.

Dawkins, Richard. *The Greatest Show on Earth – The Evidence for Evolution.* Transworld Publishers, 2009.

How Evolution Works – DonExodus2. YouTube

Judgement Day: Intelligent Design On Trial – bdw5000. YouTube.

Sagan, Carl. *Pale Blue Dot: a vision of the Human Future in Space.* The Random House Publishing Group, 1994.

This is Why Every Scientist Accepts Evolution – DonExodus2. YouTube

Chapter 3 – Foundations Built on Sand

Atheist vs Christian – Sam Harris vs William Lane Craig. YouTube

Campbell, Joseph. *The Hero with A Thousand Faces.* New. World Library, 2012.

Dawkins, Richard. *The God Delusion.* Transworld Publishers, 2006.

Is it Reasonable to Believe there is a God – Lawrence Krauss vs William Lane Craig. YouTube.

Did Jesus Even Exist? Richard Carrier. YouTube.

Hitchens, Christopher. *God is not Great*. Atlantic Books, 2007.

How Jesus Became God. Bart D. Ehrman. YouTube.

Intelligence Squared Debate: The Catholic Church is a Force for Good. Iqsquared. YouTube.

Is the New Testament Reliable? Bart D. Ehrman. YouTube

The Epic of Gilgamesh. Youtube and Wikipedia.

Unknown. *The Bible*.

What Best Explains Reality: Theism or Atheism – Frank Turek vs Christopher Hitchens

Zeitgeist: The Movie. YouTube.

Chapter 4 – 'Blind' Faith

Freud, Sigmund. The Future of an Illusion. Penguin Group, 2008.

Michael Shermer: Why People Believe Weird Things. TED talk. YouTube.

Thompson, J. Anderson, Jr. with Clare Aukofer. *Why We Believe in God(s) – A Concise Guide to The Science of Faith*. Pitchstone Publishing, 2011.

Why We Believe in Gods – Andy Thompson – American Atheists 2009. Youtube

<u>Chapter 5 – And to Dust You Shall Return</u>

Becker, Ernest. *The Denial of Death*. Free Press Paperbacks, 1997.

Death Is Not Final. Intelligence Squared Debate. YouTube.

Flight From Death: The Quest for Immortality. YouTube.

Sean Carroll on Death and the Afterlife. YouTube

Stoppard, Tom. Rosencrantz and Guildenstern are Dead. Grove Press. 1967.

The 4 Stories We Tell Ourselves About Death. Stephen Cave. TED talk. YouTube.

Wessel Zapffe, Peter. *The Last Messiah*. Philosophy Now magazine. (available online)

Chapter 6 – The Holy Grail

Csikszentmihalyi, Mihaly. *Flow: The Phycology of Happiness: The Classic Work on How to Achieve Happines*s. Harper & Row, 2002.

Kiyosaki, Robert T. *Rich Dad, Poor Dad.* Plata Publishing, 2011.

Literature – Ralph Waldo Emerson. The School of Life. YouTube.

Philosophy – Montaigne. The School of Life. YouTube.

Shadyac, Tom. *Lifes Operating Manual.* Hay House, 2013.

Tolle, Eckhart. *The Power of Now – A Guide to Spiritual Enlightenment.* Hodder & Stoughton, 2011.

Chapter 7 – Taking Control

Deida, David. *The Way of the Superior Man: A Spiritual Guide to Mastering the Challenges of Women, Work, and Sexual Desire.* Sounds True. Inc, 2004.

Freud, Sigmund. *The Ego and the Id*. Pacific Publishing Studio, 2010.

Id, Ego, Superego – Understanding An Old School Psychology Concept. Actualized.org. YouTube.

Peters, Dr Steve. *The Chimp Paradox – The Mind Management Programme for Confidence, Success and Happiness*. Ebury Publishing, 2012.

Psychotherapy – Freud. The School of Life. YouTube.

Chapter 8 – Our Driving Forces

Expanded Maslow's Hierarshy of Needs, Human Needs, Self Actualisation, Humanistic Psychology. PsycheTruth. YouTube.

Saad, Gad. *The Consuming Instinct: What Juicy Burgers, Ferraris, Pornography, and Gift Giving Reveal About Human Nature*. Prometheus Books, 2011.
Starsuckers Documentary. YouTube.

The Saad Truth_4: The Evolutionary Bases of Consumption. Gad Saad. YouTube.

Using Maslow's Hierarchy of Needs to Self-Actualize. Actualized.org. YouTube.

Chapter 9 – Be More Stoic

Aurelius, Marcus. *Meditations*. Penguin Classics, 2006.

Branden, Nathaniel. *Six Pillars of Self-Esteem*. Bantam Hardcover edition. 1994.

Epictetus. *Discourses and Selected Writings*. Penguin Classics, 2008.

Holiday, Ryan. *The Obstacle is the Way – The Timeless Art of Turning Trials into Triumph*. Portfolio / Penguin, 2014.

Ruiz, Don Miguel. *The Four Agreements: Practical Guide to Personal Freedom*. Amber-Allen Publishing. 1997.

Seneca. *Letters from a Stoic*. Penguin Classics, First published 1969.

Stoicism – Meditations by Marcus Aurelius Animated Book Review. FightMediocrity. YouTube.

Chapter 10 – Revelations

Alan Watts – What is really necessary in our life?. AlanWattsLectures. YouTube.

Frankl, Victor. *Man's Search for Meaning*. Ebury Publishing, 2004.

Gladwell, Malcolm. *Blink – The Power of Thinking without Thinking*. Penguin Books, 2005.

Green, Robert. *Mastery*. Profile Books Ltd, 2012.

Green, Robert. *The 48 Laws of Power*. Profile Books Ltd, 2000.

Kleon, Austin. *Steal Like an Artist*. Workman Publishing Company, Inc, 2012.

Malkin, Michelle. *Who Built That – Awe-inspiring Stories of American Tinkerpreneurs*. Threshold Editions/Mercury Ink, 2015.

Philosophy – Albert Camus. The School of Life. YouTube.

Philosophy – Nietzsche. The School of Life. YouTube.

Philosophy – Satre. The School of Life. YouTube.

Philosophy – Schopenhauer. The School of Life. YouTube.

Sia. Bird Set Free. From the album This Is Acting.

The Secret of Life – Alan Watts. TheJourneyofPurpose TJOP. YouTube.

Whiplash (DVD) 2015.

Printed in Great Britain
by Amazon